# Creating a Lifetime *of* Wellness

## Start Having the Life You Deserve

Aura E. Martinez

abbott press

The information, ideas, and suggestions in this book are not intended
as a substitute for professional medical advice. Before following any
suggestions contained in this book, you should consult your personal
physician. Neither the author nor the publisher shall be liable or responsible
for any loss or damage allegedly arising as a consequence of your use
or application of any information or suggestions in this book.

Abbott Press books may be ordered through booksellers or by contacting:

Abbott Press
1663 Liberty Drive
Bloomington, IN 47403
www.abbottpress.com
Phone: 1 (866) 697-5310

Because of the dynamic nature of the Internet, any web addresses or
links contained in this book may have changed since publication and
may no longer be valid. The views expressed in this work are solely those
of the author and do not necessarily reflect the views of the publisher,
and the publisher hereby disclaims any responsibility for them.

Any people depicted in stock imagery provided by Thinkstock are models,
and such images are being used for illustrative purposes only.
Certain stock imagery © Thinkstock.

ISBN: 978-1-4582-2088-2 (sc)
ISBN: 978-1-4582-2089-9 (hc)
ISBN: 978-1-4582-2087-5 (e)

Library of Congress Control Number: 2017902755

Print information available on the last page.

Abbott Press rev. date: 03/17/2017

# Table of Contents

# Message from the Author

This book is for anyone who wants a better life. So many of us are unaware of the way we are feeding ourselves mentally, emotionally, spiritually, and physically. This lack of awareness leads to a life that is far less than what we deserve. We get so caught up in everyday things that our life becomes mundane, and we neglect the things that really matter. This book is about helping you gain the awareness you need to increase your well-being every day, starting now.

A lifetime of wellness is something you can achieve. It requires daily effort, but don't let the word *effort* scare you. I know that when you hear or read that word, it may make you think of work, but work doesn't have to be a bad thing. It can be a great thing.

I want you to realize that even though we live in a society where we want everything fast and easy, greatness requires effort. Greatness is not fast and easy; it is made up of small things that we do on a daily basis. I think that the mentality of needing things to be fast and easy is what got us into trouble, and into a world where there are more people who are sick in every sense of the word—mentally, emotionally, spiritually, and physically. I am not making the claim that this is *the* reason many are sick. What I mean is that this mind-set is one of many reasons we are living unbalanced lives.

Achieving balance and having the well-being that we all strive for and need doesn't have to be difficult, nor was it ever designed to be difficult. Well-being and happiness are within your reach. This book is all about motivating you to create a lifetime of wellness. It is my hope that with this book, you will do what you have to do to claim your life and live it to the max—because you deserve it.

With love,

# How This Book Is Designed

This book is designed to tackle different areas of your life that impact your well-being. I hope to motivate you to look at your life as a whole and then tear the picture into sections so that you can look at different areas of your life and make improvements and adjustments as needed.

This book is not meant to replace any therapeutic work you may need, nor is it meant to replace any suggestions from your physician. It is meant to offer guidance so that you can have the life you want and deserve: a balanced, fulfilling life in which every morning you wake up feeling happy, vibrant, energetic, and loving life. It *is* possible to wake up feeling this way. It *is* possible to have a lifetime of wellness, but it is *you* who have to make this happen.

As you read each chapter, start thinking about your life and see where you can start implementing some of the suggestions. We are all a work in progress, so know that there is always room to improve your life in every area. If you realize while reading the book that you have failed terribly at doing something, try not to be harsh with yourself. The most important thing in life is to learn and grow and be a better version of yourself every day.

Well-being is comprised of many decisions we make on a daily basis that we may not even be aware of, as well as decisions we have made in the past. It is my hope that this book can help you gain some awareness of that. Although there are times we all want to believe that something outside of us can deliver that life, we are the ones who have to create it for ourselves.

# You Need an Oasis

It is crucial to your well-being for your home to be your oasis. You need to have a place where you can recharge your batteries, regain your sanity, and feel safe to be yourself. Your home needs to be a place you always look forward to being, a place where you can feel excited about life. Everyone needs an oasis. It's not a luxury; it's a necessity. In this hectic world we live in, an oasis is crucial for gaining the energy we need to face the jungle of the outside world.

The outside world can be a jungle because you are dealing with different people and different personalities. Sometimes they carry their own issues with them to unload onto others. We have to deal with things like work, and for some, work alone can be draining. To help you deal with all this without feeling like you're drained or going crazy, create a home that can become your oasis.

The consequences of not doing this are great. When your home is a source of chaos and stress, you'll want to be anywhere but home. This can lead to a sense of loss, because in essence, you are lost. It can be challenging to find yourself away from home, because of all the noise of the outside world. By *noise*, I mean other people's thoughts, ideas, and agendas; society's agenda; your own community; and other outside forces. When that noise does not resonate with your true essence, you cannot be your own true self. You cannot become

1

what you were designed to be. You cannot grow as a person, and growth is very much a part of your well-being.

To figure out your true happiness, you must look within, and you must do this without all the noise and influence of others. You need to feel safe. I believe our true essence is always trying to talk to us, but it cannot communicate in the midst of noise. We need that quiet oasis.

In order to function in life, you need to be able to vibrate at a high energy level. Wake up every morning expecting good from life, knowing that life is always by your side and that you are loved. Anything less than this is misery. If your home is a cause of misery, and if you would rather sleep more just because you don't want to deal with day-to-day things, then you have a big problem. I'm telling you, you can't function in a home like this. It will lead to you getting to work stressed and dealing with everything in a miserable way. You won't have much to offer to others, and they will sense that. You will carry negative energy with you everywhere you go and attract more negative things to you. One way to break from this is by making your home an oasis.

You have to create this home oasis yourself; you can't wait for someone else to do it for you. A house is just the physical brick and cement, but a home—and particularly a peaceful home—is something that you create. Make sure that it is clean and organized. Have things on display that are meaningful to you. Decorate in a way that represents who you are. Use colors that trigger a sense of happiness and calm. This is critical.

Apart from the way your home looks, if you live with someone or have your own family, it is important to create an environment of love. Make sure you express love to your loved ones. Make sure that they know they are loved in a way that makes them feel loved. To learn more, I suggest you read *The Five Love Languages* by Gary

Chapman. It provides insight about how each and every one of us feels loved differently.

If you work outside the home, find some time and energy to dedicate to your family. View that time and energy as an investment, not work. Family time should never feel like work, and you should never even think of it as work. View your family and loved ones as complementing your life and adding to your life.

We humans are social beings, and we have a need for love and attention, a need to feel needed. Make sure you provide your family with that love and attention. Trust me—it will pay you dividends. There are many investments that we should be making, and this is one of them. A broken home can be a source of anxiety for everyone, and this can happen so easily. A common cause of a broken home is neglecting one's family. No matter how stressed you are, how busy you are, or how tired you are, always make time for your family. You will be so glad you did.

Check in with yourself to see what state you are in emotionally, spiritually, and mentally. If you are not right in these three aspects, you won't have much to offer your family. To offer the best to your family, you have to be at your best. Make sure you take care of your spiritual needs. I discuss this more in the chapter "Nurture Your Soul."

Make sure you are also nurturing yourself and making time for yourself. This is crucial for your mental, emotional, and spiritual sanity. If all you are doing is taking care of others, it is only a matter of time before you feel worn out. Tending to your own needs is healthy and necessary; it's not a luxury. Even within a family, you have to retain your own individuality and nurture yourself, not just others.

One of the paths to health is checking in with yourself and making sure that you're all right. Then you will have more than enough to offer to others and be able to provide your best to your loved ones. This is the state you want to be in; it will help you create a home oasis.

I am not a relationship expert, nor am I trying to be. I am a Wellness and Life Coach, and as an expert in this area, I understand how crucial our love lives are to our well-being. Please don't take your husband, wife, or companion for granted. One of the many reasons families break up is because one of the two parties feels taken for granted or that his or her needs are not being met. By taking your husband, wife, or companion for granted, you are neglecting your home, because a home is built by love, nurture, attention, and effort.

Make sure that every day, you are winning your partner's affection and love. Keep doing the things that made him or her fall in love with you. Make sure that your partner knows that you love, desire, and need him or her. Make time for your spouse or companion, and make him or her feel special. Turn off your phone when you are together. Do whatever it takes to make that person love you more. It is not just the other person's responsibility to make the relationship work; it is yours as well.

Do your part, and I guarantee it will have a ripple effect on everything in your life. Your husband, wife, or companion will not feel the need to look outside the relationship for what he or she needs because you are providing it, and home will be an oasis that your spouse or companion will want to come home to. We are emotional beings. If we can create this feeling in our spouses/companions, home will be the first and only place they think of when they need to recharge their batteries.

A home where there is chaos contributes to disease—mental, emotional, spiritual, and with time even physical disease. Stress is no joke, and the last thing you need is to have more stress at home. A home where there is chaos creates a sense of emptiness, and that sense of emptiness can lead to a sense of loss. Loss is not a good feeling, nor were you designed to feel this way. This feeling can make you look in all the wrong places for ways to fulfill your needs.

Looking outside will not be of much help. There is no place like home for fulfilling your needs. You must have a safe haven, and what better place for that than your home? Your home was designed to be your oasis. Anything less than an oasis is not a home; when this is the case, changes need to be made. Remember that you play a role in making those changes happen. Don't leave it all for the other person.

Making your home your oasis should be your priority. Your health depends on it. This is the last place you see at night and the first place you see in the morning, so make it a place you look forward to being.

## Things to Think About

- Is your home currently an oasis for you?
- If not, what do you think is contributing to it not being an oasis?
- What can you do right now to make it the safe haven that you need it to be?
- If you live with your family, are you doing your part to dedicate time to them? Do you show them love in a way that makes them feel loved?
- Do you frequently check in with yourself to know the state you're in mentally, emotionally and spiritually?
- Are you nurturing yourself?
- Are you taking responsibility for making your home an oasis?

# Know What Your Needs Are

**N**ow I would like to discuss the importance of knowing what your needs are in terms of creating a lifetime of wellness. When you understand what your needs are, you have a road map for your life. It is crucial to understand who you are and what you're all about. When you have that level of understanding, you can finally attain the happiness that you need and crave.

Not knowing what your needs are can lead you to make choices that are not right for you. The choices you make may seem right at the moment, but you end up realizing that they were the wrong choices after all. For example, if you don't know what your needs are in terms of a relationship—and for this example, I mean *relationship* in a romantic sense—you may end up choosing anyone or settling for something less than what you need and deserve.

If you know you need attention, as I think every woman does—and by this I don't mean a guy dedicating himself to you 24/7, but simply letting you know that he cares, is present, and misses you when you're apart—and you notice that the guy you are seeing doesn't provide that, then you know that guy is not right for you. If this isn't so important to you, that's fine, as long as you and your partner are on the same page. Knowing what your needs are allows you to be upfront and clear about what you need, which in turn allows you to attract what you want.

When you know what your needs are, you know what you cannot compromise on. If there's one thing you don't ever want to compromise on—and I write this from personal experience—it's your well-being. The moment you feel drained, the moment you feel exhausted, the moment you feel sad, depressed, any of those negative feelings, you are already compromising your well-being. This is why it is important for you to know and understand what your needs are.

The same is true in your work life. Not every job is meant for everyone. There are certain jobs that some people can handle while others cannot. Understanding what you are willing to handle and what you are not willing to handle gives you a road map as to what kind of employment you can apply for. For instance, when I went for an interview to be a flight attendant, I knew from the moment I went to Atlanta for that interview that this job could very well be for me. I'm not the kind to get homesick. I love adventure, and I love the idea that one minute I'm in one place and the next I'm in another. On top of that, I like being around people, and I love airplanes. Because of all this, I knew I could handle that job—I just knew it. On the other hand, if you are someone who needs to be at your house every night and have a regular schedule, an inflight job would not be for you. Know what your needs are.

It's important to know what your needs are even when it comes to friendship. Ask yourself what you're looking for in a friend. I know that I need people who are ambitious and have great things going for themselves, because people like that motivate me to want to be better. You may have loyalty at the top of your list. We all need people who love themselves, and this is a big one; people who cannot love themselves and who are full of jealousy and envy, they don't have much to offer you in the way of spiritual, mental, and emotional energy. We're all just energy at the end of the day, and it benefits you to be around people who are operating on a high energy level and want great things out of life.

I'm a believer that we become like the people we hang around with and talk to. This is why being careful who you surround yourself with is so important. Knowing what you need from your social circle is going to help you understand the kind of person you must become. If you want to surround yourself with positive people, if you want to be around people who are ambitious and have things going for them, you have to be the first one to be positive. You have to be the first one with things going for you. You can't have one thing without the other. You can't have the life you want and need without that deep understanding of yourself.

Once again, I believe that each and every one of us deserves a purposeful, fulfilling life. In order to have that life, you need to have a great understanding of who you are. Having that great understanding means that you know what your needs are and don't compromise those needs.

How can you find out what your needs are? You really have to dig within yourself, because you're the only one who knows. Don't allow anyone else to tell you what your needs are, because the moment you start listening to other people's voices, you lose your true self. The way to be your true self is by listening to your true essence, which is your soul. You have to ask yourself the following:

- What are the things I know beyond a shadow of a doubt that I need?
- Why do I need these things?
- Why are these things so important to me?
- What is it about these things that if I don't have them, I feel empty or lost or as though something is missing?

Your answers will solidify your understanding of your *why*. It's what drives you to do the things you want to do, so figure out why it is that you can't be without that need. What is it that makes it a need? What does that need represent for you?

I'll use myself as an example. In terms of a romantic relationship, I need attention, not because I'm needy, but because it is a way for me to feel loved by the guy. When the guy takes the time to be there for me and let me know that he misses me, that is a form of love to me. It's a sign that I am loved.

One thing I would like to clarify is that your needs and the reasons behind them don't have to make sense to anyone else. They just have to make sense to you. That's what matters. I write this because you need to give yourself the power to say to yourself, "This is how I am, this is what I need, this is why I need it, and so be it." Whether other people are accepting or understanding is irrelevant.

You have more power than you think. At the end of the day, you go to sleep and wake up to yourself, not to someone else. Think about it this way: Are other people paying your bills? Are other people providing for you? No. You are providing for yourself. You are paying your own bills. You have to sleep and wake up to yourself. So the only person who has to understand you, the only person who has to be accepting of who you are, what your needs are, and what you are all about is you. The more you look for other people's approval of who you are and what you need, the more lost you're going to feel. Nobody has the answers to your life but you.

Take several pieces of paper or a journal and write down some of the following things:

- From a romantic relationship I need ...
- For me to have that fabulous job, I need ...
- For my social circle, I need ...

- In my home, I need …
- In my life, I need …

Be as specific as you need to be. Then, right next to the needs that you have for the different categories, write why you have those needs. What is it that make those needs important for you? Why is it that you cannot be without those needs? What is it that makes you feel that something is missing without that need? Why is that? Be as specific as possible.

I find writing things down very helpful; it makes your thoughts and ideas more real when you see them in writing. There is no right or wrong way of doing this; it is for your eyes only. If you want, you can share your list with someone you trust.

While you're asking these questions, be sure to ask yourself what you need from yourself. Answers might include love, compassion, attention, or putting yourself as a priority. So many of us, especially women, are so good at giving to others and being attentive to others' needs that we forget ourselves in the process. This is not healthy. If it continues for too long, you will end up feeling resentful, and that resentment can build until you are almost the opposite of what you were. Rather than having a balance between giving to yourself and to others, you may end up wanting to give to yourself only, because you feel you have given enough. Establish a balance now before you get to that point. Understand what you need from yourself and start meeting those needs.

It is crucial for you to know what your needs are and why. It will help diminish or keep at bay the kinds of people you do not need in your life. It will help you make a better decision in terms of what you need from a companion, friends, and everything else in life because you're coming from a place of wisdom, knowing who you are, and knowing what you're all about. Your choices will come from who you really are, which is your true essence. When you live from your true essence, you start to be in alignment. Alignment makes you centered, and when you are centered, you feel balance.

Knowing what your needs are helps you set your priorities. You don't waste time on things that don't matter to you. You don't waste time on relationships that aren't fruitful for you. It's almost as if you go forward in life with a sense of determination and purpose. That's important.

Take some time now to discover your needs in every area of your life. Look at the time you take to do this as "me time," a very precious period of getting to know yourself better and improving in every area of your life. You are worth the time and attention.

## Things to Think About

- If your life isn't the way you want it to be, ask yourself why.
- Find out what area of your life is not fulfilling and ask yourself what your needs are in that area.
- Have a journal and set aside some "me time" when you can figure out what your needs are without any interruptions or distractions.
- Make a list of your needs in a romantic relationship, in friendship, at work, and from yourself. Ask yourself why you have that need and why it is important to you.
- Get as detailed as possible with all that you write. The more you understand yourself, the better. This is for your eyes only, unless you want to share this with someone you trust.

# Be Loving Toward Yourself

The first person you must love, the first person you must care for, the first person you must respect is yourself. You may think that if you had someone who loved you, if you met The One, you could be loving toward yourself. When you wait for someone else to love you first before you can be loving toward yourself, you are jeopardizing your well-being on so many levels. You are compromising your self-love. This puts you in a weak position—and on top of that, this quality isn't attractive. It will repel healthy people and attract those who feed off your low self-esteem, like psychopaths and abusers.

You need to be loving toward yourself first. When you are loving toward yourself, you set healthy boundaries, including what you won't tolerate from others and how much of something you are willing to put up with. When you have healthy boundaries, you don't allow disrespect.

When you're not loving toward yourself, the choices you make will not be the best for you. It is almost as if, emotionally and mentally, you are hindered from making choices that are in your best interest. When you don't love yourself, you look for that love in all the wrong places, and some of those places can get you into trouble. Love has to come from you first.

Lack of love for yourself will extend into all areas of your life—to your eating habits, your spending habits, the language you use toward yourself and others, your house/home, and your mind-set. Using eating habits as an example, when you don't love yourself, you don't care what you put in your mouth. You don't care to make the effort to cook yourself a healthy meal. You don't care if what you're eating is damaging you. You don't care to change your eating habits if you have an illness. You just don't care. This will have long-term consequences that only feed low self-esteem. If you're not careful, an illness can depress your body. I believe an illness can make us stronger if we allow ourselves to grow as a result, but it won't happen if we don't have love for ourselves.

One of the worst things you can do when feeling sad is go shopping. You end up buying things you don't need just to fill a void that you have. At the end, you have things you do not need occupying space that could have been used for something else. You also end up with less money—money that could have been used for something else. When you feel sad or bored, avoid stores altogether. This way, you avoid the temptation to spend. The last thing you need in a case like this is to also feel bad because you have a debt you cannot pay.

Lack of love for yourself extends to the language you use toward yourself and others. Each and every one of us has an internal dictionary with words, verbs, and nouns we use to describe ourselves and others on a daily basis. When you're not loving toward yourself, the nouns, verbs and words you use are not healthy. Non-loving words include the following:

- ugly
- horrible
- stupid
- I can't

- ridiculous
- limitation
- hate

These are words you do not want to use toward yourself because they color and shape your world. When you use words like *stupid*, *ugly*, or *I can't*, you are mentally incapacitating yourself. If these are the words you are using to describe others, take a good look at yourself and check your self-esteem. Ask yourself if this is how you feel about yourself but are projecting onto others. This is one of the reasons you first need to be loving toward yourself, because you can only give what you have.

Our physical environment also reflects who we are. When you are not loving toward yourself, you won't really care what your physical environment looks like. Most likely your house will look chaotic, and that is a reflection of how you feel. If you live with other people, they too will feel the chaos, and this will affect your relationship with them. Their inner energy will change, making them feel anxious. When someone feels anxious, they can only attract more negative states and situations. Your home is really the center of your life. If it is chaotic, everything else will be chaotic as well.

I believe that by not being loving toward yourself, you become a weight for others. How so? The way you feel and treat yourself emanates in everything that you do, your interaction with others, how you make others feel, etc. When you lack respect and love for yourself, you can't give true respect and love to others. It's almost as if you're making others responsible for making up for that lack. That is not right; no one is responsible for your life but you. You don't want to be a weight to others. You want to be a person who adds to others, and you can only do this by loving yourself.

Imagine this for a moment: Because you are not being loving

14

toward yourself, you only eat junk food, and as a result of doing this, you start to develop a chronic disease. Even with your chronic disease, you still don't take care of yourself, and that is also hurting those around you. It is painful to see a loved one ill, and caring for loved ones can be burdensome when they can't care for themselves. This is why I encourage you to love yourself enough to want to take care of yourself now. You don't have to wait to be sick to start taking care of yourself.

When you're not loving toward yourself, this will extend to your mind-set. Oh, the mind! It is one of the most powerful organs we have. It is the body's computer. It stores who you are, because this is where memories are formed. It determines your ability to speak and sends messages to your body. The mind is truly the command station and plays a huge role in who you are. When you are not loving toward yourself, you're shaping your mind into doing things that are not conducive to your well-being. You make choices that are not good for you. You get into relationships that are not healthy for you. One of the ways to start controlling your mind-set is to start loving yourself.

Why do I bring up examples of what not loving yourself can do to you? I want you to fully understand the importance of loving yourself. I want you to understand the high price you pay when you do not love yourself. I believe that deep understanding creates true and lasting changes. When you are not loving toward yourself, your own dictionary and your vocabulary will reflect this. When you use limiting words about yourself, it will affect your actions, because you mentally have already incapacitated yourself with your way of thinking.

So how do you start being loving toward yourself? The first step is valuing your body. Your physical body is your real home and your real vehicle. It is because of your body that you are able to go from point A to point B. You can start being loving toward your body by getting enough sleep, drinking enough water, eating right, being physically active, making sure you know all the medications you are taking and their side effects, and listening to your body.

You are loving toward yourself when you use positive, loving words like *great, smart, intelligent, awesome, I will,* and *beautiful.* These are words to start using now and on a daily basis to describe yourself, the things that you have had a hard time accepting about yourself, or a situation that you have been struggling with. Believe it or not, when you use negative words to describe a situation that you are struggling with, you create resistance. When you create resistance, the situation that you don't like will continue. When instead you use positive words, you accept the situation as is, and this opens up the possibility for growth.

You are loving toward yourself when you create a home of peace and order. Remember, you *need* peace and order in your home and in your personal space. I said it before and I will say it again so that it can be drilled in your mind that your home is the center of your life. When that is not in order, when that is a source of chaos, it will spill into every area of your life. As human beings, we tend to carry our problems with us, and this is because we are emotional beings. Make your home a source of peace, love, and order. You owe this to yourself.

You are loving toward yourself when you take responsibility for your life. The truth is that no one can really give you the life that you want, nor should you give that responsibility to someone else. That is unfair to them and to you. How can anyone else really know what makes you happy? That is something that only you truly know. You need to take charge of your life; by you doing that, you are making yourself happy and giving yourself the power to believe you can create the life you want.

Part of being loving toward yourself is learning to see and know your own value. Whether you realize it or not, you are a very valuable person. You have so much to offer to others that is unique to you. When you realize this not just with your mind but with your heart as well, the way you treat yourself changes. Your own self-value won't change whether others see that value or not. Other people are not the ones who are going to provide you with your value. Things will not provide you with value. You provide yourself with that value.

You are the one who sets your own value, and you find your own value within you. When you notice this and embrace it, you will feel something shifting deep within you. When you value yourself, other people's opinions won't matter. What others say won't matter. Whether you have someone who sees your value or not won't matter. At the end of the day, the only person who matters and really needs to see your value is you. The whole world can tell you how wonderful and talented you are, but if you don't see that, other people's words and beliefs won't matter.

You are loving toward yourself when you learn to forgive yourself for your mistakes. This is a hard one, and it's something I have struggled with so much. I tend to be the queen of being hard on myself. I blame myself for things not working out, so I understand if forgiving yourself can seem difficult. The truth is that forgiveness leads to releasing yourself.

When you forgive yourself for the mistakes you have made, you open yourself up to the lessons that life wants to bring to you. You open yourself up to being the person that you are meant to be. You open yourself up to healing. Not healing from past hurts leads to more hurt. It leads to you subconsciously pushing away any good that can come your way. This is why forgiveness is so important for your whole well-being.

There are many little details that are not so small because of the big role they play on our well-being, and this certainly is one of them. From personal experience, I can tell you that when I didn't forgive myself for some silly mistake I made, I ended up making *more* mistakes, pushing away even more of the goodness that life has for me.

You forgive yourself by recognizing what you did wrong and the emotions you are feeling as a result of that mistake. Despite the way you feel and the mistake that you made, you say to yourself that you still love yourself. I suggest that you find a method that works for you in order to start the forgiveness process. There are so many methods out there, including tapping (also known as EFT), hypnosis (which thanks to my soul mate friend Dawn I started doing and I love it), and meditation. By all means, if you need to and can afford it, see a therapist or a psychologist. This is not a sign of weakness; it's a sign of strength. It takes strength and courage to admit that you need help and then seek that help. We all need help from time to time, so don't be afraid to seek it out. Anything that strengthens your emotional and mental well-being is worth it.

Being loving toward yourself is not a luxury, it is a necessity. It is a must for your well-being. You can't afford not to be loving toward yourself, because not doing so would be costly. As you have read, there are many ways to start being loving toward yourself right now. Everyone is different, and so you may have a slightly different way of giving more love to yourself. Just remember that you owe this to yourself.

I would like to add that when you are loving toward yourself, you will be able to be loving toward others. I wrote it before and I will write it again: you can only give what you have, so if you don't have much love for yourself, you won't have much love for others either. So I challenge you now, if you haven't yet, to do loving things for yourself, like taking care of your body, listening to your soul and body, being gentle with yourself, and doing things that make you happy.

## Things to Think About

- The first person you must love, care for, and respect is yourself.
- Don't wait for someone else to love you first before you love yourself.
- Not being loving toward yourself has several consequences, including attracting the wrong people in your life and looking for love in all the wrong places. This affects every other area of your life.
- Start loving yourself by valuing your body, by having a positive dictionary that you use to describe yourself and others, and by creating a home of peace and order. Your home reflects how you feel.
- You are also loving toward yourself when you take responsibility for your life, see your own value, and forgive yourself for your mistakes.
- Loving yourself is not a luxury; it is a necessity.

# Strive to Be Loving Toward Others

There is something so gratifying about giving love to others. You exist in this world to add to people's lives—that's how meaningful you are. When you are loving toward others, you attract people into your life. We are attracted to beautiful, positive things, and so being loving toward others makes you beautiful. This is such a quick and free way to add beauty to yourself. When you are loving toward others, you also become a magnet for positive opportunities. I believe this world needs more people to be loving toward others.

There are many ways to be loving toward others. One of the simplest is smiling. You never know how someone else's day went—your smile might be the thing that brings a bit of joy to them. There is a bonus: when you smile at others, you are also adding more health into your life. I believe that although we are ultimately responsible for our own happiness, we should make it a goal to add joy to other people's lives, not misery.

Another simple way to be loving toward others is by being polite. Saying "please" and "thank you" will never go out of style. This is a way to show others that you appreciate their service and their time. Don't ever come from a place of entitlement. Even if you paid for a service and even if others are just doing their job, it is nice to show that you appreciate what they do.

Be loving toward your family and loved ones. Unfortunately, there are some who take their family for granted, and this should not happen. Your family and loved ones are among your best assets. They are the ones who will be there for you through thick and thin. If you are married and have kids, these are the people you see day in and day out, so it behooves you to be loving toward them. It is part of creating that oasis in your home that I discussed earlier. What better way to create harmony in your home than to be loving toward your family? You will create good energy in the home, making it an appealing place to be. Remind your loved ones often that you love them. Say how much they mean to you. Love them the way they need to be loved.

Be loving toward your colleagues at work. The truth is that each and every one of us has a story. We all have baggage, and some people's may be heavier than others. Because everyone has a story, you never know what someone else is going through. You don't know someone else's struggle. You don't know what the other person is feeling at the time; something as simple as a smile and a "good morning" may make that person's day.

We are all energy, and on a daily basis we are exchanging energy. Make it your goal at work to give off positive energy to others. I do understand that as human beings, when we have a lot going on in our personal life, we tend to bring all that everywhere we go. Do your best to leave your home problems at home. The moment you step out of your house and close the door behind you, leave what's going on at home behind that door. If you're lucky enough to have a job that you love, this is your chance to enjoy yourself and relax rather than bring all your personal problems to work. Besides, you don't want your personal business to be all over the place and in public.

If you are going out on a date or even hanging out with friends, a way for you to be loving toward them is by putting down your cell phone and giving your attention to the person in front of you. It seems like we live in a world where more and more people are disconnected, and technology plays a role in this. The most precious moment that you have is your moment with another, and so give that person in front of you your attention. Make sure you are not on the phone having a conversation with someone else while you are having a conversation with a person in front of you. It's rude, and it shows a lack of respect. When you are going out with someone, give that person your attention.

Be loving toward those who serve you at a restaurant, bookstore, supermarket, anywhere and everywhere you go. When you talk to others, talk from a place of gratitude. Know that you are lucky to be able to sit and dine at that restaurant, not that the waiter is lucky to be able to serve you. Know that you are lucky to be able to buy a book; it is a luxury and an opportunity to grow your knowledge. Know that you are lucky to be able to buy food at the supermarket to feed and nurture your body.

No matter what you're buying or what service you're paying for, always speak from a place of gratitude. When you do this, your attitude changes. You are more positive and more delightful, and others will be happy to serve you. It all comes down to this: what you give is what you get back.

Being loving toward others doesn't take much effort. The world is in need of that, and you never know whose day you may make with your kind words and gestures. There is something about being loving toward others that brings happiness to you. It draws positive people and beautiful things to you. You get what you give, so make sure that you give love, goodness, and good energy to others. Start thinking of ways to be loving toward your family members, your colleagues at work, the people you interact with often, and even strangers. The more love you give, the more love you will feel.

## Things to Think About

- Make it your goal to be loving toward others on a daily basis.

- There are many ways to be loving toward others, like saying "please," "thank you," and "good morning"; by smiling at others; and by coming from a place of gratitude.

- When you are going into a store or anywhere you go where a service is being provided to you, know that you are lucky to be able to afford that service and treat those who provide it with respect, not a sense of entitlement.

- When you are spending time with someone, give that person your full attention. Put the phone aside. Don't text with someone else; this is a form of disrespect to the person in front of you.

- Remind those you love that you love them and think of them.

# Define Your Happiness

**H**appiness on a basic level is standard for everyone to a certain extent. In order to be happy we all need certain basic things like love, acceptance, freedom, and meaningful relationships. However, because we are all unique and different, different things will make us happy.

So what is the definition of happiness? It depends on your values and what is most important to you and your true essence. You cannot get the answer from someone else. You have to look within to define it. If you're wondering, "What if I don't know how to define this? How about if I don't really know what makes me happy?" my response is that at a certain level, you *do* know what makes you happy. You have to start listening to yourself more in order to know what it is. Your soul will indicate to you what to do and what makes you happy, since your soul is your true essence. This is why no one else can define your happiness, only you.

What happens when you define your own happiness is that you start reaching within for your own inner guidance. You start to really create the life you were meant to live. You start living your life on your own terms. This is the best way to live your life. Align yourself according to your true values and beliefs. When you start living life based on what makes you happy, you see how fabulous life can be. Life starts to feel fabulous because your life is based on the true you.

You realize that there is nothing like being your true self without any worries as to what someone else will think or say.

When you live other people's definition of happiness rather than your own, you deny yourself true happiness. You deny yourself being who you are supposed to be. You kill little by little your true essence. Eventually, you will be no good for others. If you cannot make yourself happy, how can you make anyone else happy? You start attracting situations, people, and things that are not congruent with your true self. These situations, people, and things don't make you truly happy. You lose your sense of self in the process, and this keeps you from living the life you were meant to live.

I can tell you from personal experience that it is awful to feel lost. You feel so empty, and you subconsciously look outside of yourself for someone who can rescue you. The problem with this is that nobody can rescue you; you can only rescue yourself. If you're lucky, you may have good friends who remind you of this fact the way my friends do for me.

You rescue yourself by realizing that you are the one who has power over your life. You rescue yourself by taking responsibility for your life. You rescue yourself by not looking outside of yourself for your happiness. You rescue yourself by defining what happiness means to you. You rescue yourself by being open to your own inner wisdom. I learned the hard way that you also rescue yourself by surrendering. You surrender yourself to what is instead of resisting. You allow things to be.

Make yourself responsible for your own happiness regardless of the outcome of events— whether or not someone speaks to you, a relationship works, you get the job, or anything else. When you tie your happiness to the outcome of a situation, you delay your happiness, and you're not putting yourself in the driver's seat of your life. It's as if you're in the passenger seat watching your life go by while allowing something or someone else to decide where you will go. When you allow this, of course you will not get the things you want in life. Of course you will feel unhappy. Of course you will feel lost, because you are not making yourself responsible for your life.

Making yourself responsible for your life involves taking the time to understand what makes you happy. You need to have stillness. Make space in your life every day for stillness. This stillness will provide you with answers to what you really want and need in life.

Live the life you want and not the life that others want. Do this regardless of whether or not it makes sense to others. Things that don't make any sense now start to make sense over time. My suggestion would be to write down what you see for yourself in your life. If you could do anything, what would it be? Let your imagination flow, and don't be ashamed if you start dreaming big things. You were meant to dream big things.

Even if what you dream seems small to others, it is not what others think about you that matters, it is what you think and feel about yourself. No one has the right to judge or define you. It is you who define yourself. Make sure that your definition of happiness is something that comes from you, not a source outside of you.

I remember when I believed that having a relationship and meeting the right one was the source of happiness. Although it is normal to have that need for love and to cultivate a healthy relationship with someone, it was putting me in a situation where I was constantly feeling hurt. When things didn't work out with a guy, I would immediately feel sad and start looking at things from a negative perspective. When I make my source of happiness serving others and using the gifts I was given to add to other people's life as well as my own, I was able to create happiness on a daily basis. I learned the hard way that happiness comes from within you, not a source outside of you. When you rely on outside sources, you may be bitterly disappointed.

The bonus of looking within you to define your own happiness is that others will be drawn to you because of the positive energy that emanates from you. You will draw the right people and situations to you, and you will start having the life you have always wanted. Of course, outside things can make us happy, but we cannot rely on those things to be *the* source of our happiness. We have to be willing to be happy even without those things. Allow outside things to *add* to your happiness. Knowing your own value and mastering the art of letting go helps you avoid making outside sources responsible for your happiness.

Think about the things you do that make you happy. Make it a daily habit to do those things. This is one way to train yourself to be happy; you are training your mind to feel and think that way. This also aids in defining what happiness means to you, because happiness comes in many different ways for everyone. What makes someone else happy may not make you happy and vice versa.

Our emotions are like the temperature of our soul. Just as you would use a thermometer to measure your body temperature, your emotions measure where you are in life. They measure the thoughts you have at the present time. So as you start defining your own happiness, pay attention to the way they make you feel. Your feelings will indicate to you whether you are on the right track or not. One thing I would like for you to keep in mind is to know the difference between when something doesn't feel right because it's not right for you and when something feels scary to you, which can also make you feel not right, because whatever it is that you want is something new to you. It's important to pay attention to all this. This will help you define your own happiness. It is important that you know that only you have the answer as to what makes you happy.

One of the things I would like to encourage is not feeling ashamed, afraid, and guilty if your definition of happiness does not sit well with others. If painting makes you happy but your family doesn't agree, remember that you are the one living your life. No one else is living it for you.

The truth is, it doesn't matter if others agree with your definition of happiness, as long as you are not doing anything that hurts others or yourself. The moment you carry a dictionary other than your own and for as long as you are living other people's dreams and their life, you will never be happy. Not being happy compromises your well-being in every sense. Happiness is essential for achieving balance in every area of your life. When one area of your life is off, it can throw off every other area of your life. This is why balance is important.

When you compromise your well-being in any way, you walk through life feeling miserable, frustrated, and negative. It is very important to break away from what other people think, not because you want to go against them, but because what matters is what you are saying and thinking—what *your* true essence is saying and thinking. Once you start listening to your true essence, life will start coming together, and you will start feeling a sense of peace and abundance.

You may start questioning where all this comes from. These feelings came to you because you started listening to your own self and what truly makes you happy. You started defining your life. When you define your life, you will have the right mind-set. You are setting your mind according to what is right for you. When you do what is right for you, you do things that matter to your soul, and you can be your most productive self. You start being more in alignment with who you are.

When you are in alignment, you attract the right people into your life, subconsciously pushing away those who are wrong for you.

The more you do things that you love, the happier you will feel. The happier you feel, the more goodness you will experience.

To start defining your own happiness, I would suggest that you sit down with yourself and set a time when you are not talking to anyone, you are not hearing noises, you are by yourself, and you don't have anything to do or anything that can interrupt you. Start asking yourself important questions. It is so important to ask questions, because when you ask questions, you are going to get answers.

A colleague of mine told me that the mind is like a Google search engine. You ask a question and it will give you an answer. If you ask a negative question, you will get a negative answer. If you ask a positive question, you will get a positive answer. The mind works in this exact way so be mindful of the questions you ask yourself.

Let your imagination flow as you imagine yourself doing all the things you love. What would those be? What is one thing you could do right now that would make you happy? What are some of the things that when you think about them, they make you feel happy? I suggest that you also think about things that make you feel the opposite. It is important to know what makes you feel miserable and the reason for this so you know what to do less of.

Sometimes the reason we feel so miserable in life is because we keep doing over and over the very thing that makes us unhappy, and we don't even realize it. This is why awareness and understanding are so powerful. Awareness sheds light where there is darkness, and understanding provides you with the reason as to why whatever happened occurred in the first place. You need both awareness and understanding.

Take the time to define your own happiness. Understand what you value and what makes your soul light up. Understand and know what you want out of life. Do not allow anyone else to define happiness for you. Their definition of happiness may be different from yours because you are different individuals. You want to start living life on your terms. When you can define happiness, this is exactly what you are doing.

## Things to Think About

- For your well-being, it is crucial that you start defining your own happiness.
- What may make someone else happy may not make you happy, and vice versa.
- Listening to your true essence is what will help you find your own definition of happiness.
- Once you know what makes you happy, you will be able to align your life accordingly, attracting the things and people that you need and want.
- If you can't make yourself happy, you can't be any good to anyone.

# Nurture Your Soul

I think we all know that we need to nurture our body, and most of us do nurture our mind, but there is one part of us that many neglect and may not realize the value of nurturing it. Neglecting this other part of you can be disastrous for both your body and mind. This other part I would encourage you to nurture on a daily basis is your soul.

When you nurture your soul, you are nurturing your true essence. Nurturing your true essence brings a sense of fulfillment that is crucial to your well-being. When your soul is hungry, you feel a sense of emptiness, and this can lead you to make the wrong choices in your life. Depending on the extent of the emptiness, it can lead to addictions, such as alcohol, drugs, overeating, and compulsive shopping. You will look outside of you to fulfill this void, and that is the worst thing you can do. Nothing outside of you can fill a void caused by your lack of nurturing.

Nurturing your soul is like nurturing a child. Apart from making sure that children are well fed and that they go to school, you also make sure they are happy and that they are loved, so you play with them, make them laugh, hug them and kiss them, and make sure they feel safe. You must do exactly the same thing with your true essence.

The way you make your soul feel safe is to protect it from harm. You don't put yourself in situations where your soul will feel sad.

You do things that make your true essence light up with joy; you will know what those things are based on the way you feel. Your emotions are like a thermometer. As a thermometer measures body temperature, emotions measure the state of your soul.

Surround yourself with people who are genuinely loving and caring and who can see the precious being that you are. This will make your soul happy. When you do this, you are actually loving yourself, and you are taking responsibility for your own well-being.

When you nurture your true essence, you are basically getting yourself a life. You are taking steps to make yourself happy, and you are listening to yourself. You are making yourself responsible for your own well-being.

There is a domino effect to this simple act of nurturing your soul. You will start seeing different sides of yourself that you didn't even know were there. You will be curious to learn about your fascinating self. You will grow in self-esteem as you realize how fabulous you always were and still are. As your self-esteem starts to rise, others will take notice, and this will draw more people to you.

Your mind will shift to a positive outlook as you grow in self-love, and this will help you create healthy boundaries for yourself. When you have healthy boundaries, you don't allow disrespect from others. You don't allow mistreatment. Your demeanor changes, and this speaks for itself in regards to how you feel about yourself.

When you nurture your soul, you have so much more to give. This is exactly the place you want to be; you always want to give your best to others. You want to be that person others feel drawn to, but for this to happen, you must nurture your soul. You can only give what you have, and if you don't first make sure that you fill yourself up with love, care, and attention, you won't have much of these things to give to others. This is why it is necessary to help and love yourself before you help and love others.

The consequences of not nurturing your soul are many. You have a sense of emptiness, and you have no idea where it is coming from. You don't have a deep sense of appreciation toward yourself because you haven't seen the jewels you have hidden inside you. Relationships can be severed because we are all energy, and when our energy isn't right, we don't give our best to others. Even worse, we expect them to fill needs that we should be filling up ourselves.

When you feel empty, your mind only looks at all the things that are wrong in your life. All the things that are not working for you are magnified, and this intensifies negative feelings that you have. This creates a cycle of negativity that takes you nowhere, and it snowballs into nothing good. You cannot afford to be in this state. It is too expensive to your well-being. Anything that makes you feel sadness, anger, resentfulness, worry, and any negative feeling just wears you out. It drains your energy in every way. Anything that drains your energy creates a vicious cycle that just goes on and on.

There are many ways to nurture your soul. Start by listening to yourself. What are some of the things you are curious to learn or do? Whatever sparks your interest and curiosity, start doing it. That may be your soul speaking to you. You may discover something about yourself that you didn't even know you had within you. At the end of the day, you are doing something that makes you happy. You are doing it for yourself, and you will notice your self-esteem rising. It feels good to do something for yourself. Do something every day that brings joy to you. Do something that makes you feel loved.

There are many things you can do that will help you feel loved. Let me just tell you that when you feel loved, it is your soul that feels loved. This has ripple effects for you. Wear clothes that make you feel beautiful or handsome. Do things that make you feel good. Make sure you watch things that make you laugh. Laughter is so healthy for you.

Learn to listen to yourself. Your true essence is always communicating with you through your emotions. When you feel good after doing something, your soul is telling you that you should be doing more of the same. When doing something makes you feel sad or angry, your soul is telling you to stay away from that.

On a daily basis, we get feedback about the things we are doing, but we tend to ignore it. Start paying attention to your emotions. Start paying attention to how your body feels. Start paying attention to what your true essence is telling you. You already have an inner map telling you where to go to find total happiness and well-being. Only you know how to read that map, so start listening to yourself. The more you listen, the happier you will be. Others don't necessarily have the key to your happiness, but you absolutely do.

The way you start listening to yourself is by looking within you and giving yourself some quiet time. Give yourself permission to believe in your own advice and intuition. Don't pay much mind to what others are thinking or saying. When you pay attention to other people's voices, you are actually shutting down your own voice, and when you do that you can never really know yourself.

Once you start paying attention to your soul, I guarantee you will see great results in every area of your life and will be happy beyond measure. Start living authentically and be true to who you are. This means you're living according to what makes you happy. You are living your dreams and your life according to you. Living authentically means that you are living according to your values, not someone else's values. You do and have things because that's what you want, not what someone else wants. You are on your journey, and you have an understanding of the journey you are on, regardless of whether or not others understand.

When you don't live authentically and true to yourself, you do deny yourself and the world the gift of you. You were designed to be *you*, whoever that *you* is. Your likes and dislikes, your wants, your needs, and your taste are what make you unique. Strive to be yourself regardless of whether or not others understand you. When you try to be like others, it's as if you are denying your soul, and your soul is your true essence. When you reject your true essence, there is no way you can be truly happy. Part of being happy is being your true self. Don't reject yourself by being someone you are not.

When you are your true self, you are living according to what your soul needs. You know exactly what to do to make yourself happy. In essence, your soul is your inner guide. You already have a map that shows you where you need to go in life. Now you need to look within to get the guide so that you can interpret that map. When you look within, you will get the answers you need. No one is better qualified to tell you what you need but your true essence. The more you nurture your soul, the more answers you will get.

Start thinking of ways you can nurture your soul. What are some things that give you peace and happiness? What are some things you can start doing that would be loving to you? If you feel any sense of anger or frustration, what are these emotions trying to tell you? What are some of the things that bring joy to you? Your soul communicates to you through your emotions. Don't ignore them, and you will find a wealth of knowledge that will serve you well.

## Things to Think About

- Your soul is an essential part of who you are.
- You nurture your soul by paying attention to it, by paying attention to your emotions, and by doing things that spark your curiosity and interest.

- When you do things that spark your curiosity and interest, you will learn things about yourself that perhaps you didn't even know before.
- Nurturing your soul is like caring for a child, only the person you are caring for is your true essence.
- Think about ways you can start taking care of this part of you now.

# Nurture Your Body

Your body is the most precious home and vehicle you will ever own. It is the house of your soul—your true essence—and it is the vehicle that takes you from point A to point B. Because of this, it only makes sense to take care of your health. The state of your body is what will determine the state of your life. This becomes very evident when you are sick.

The state of your body determines what work you can do—and if you can even work. Compromised health can deter you from working, especially if your job is very physical. The state of your body determines both your emotional and physical energy. When we don't feel well, we don't have much energy, and this affects how we feel emotionally. There is no way to feel happy when we are tired. Our physical health is directly linked to our emotional health and vice versa.

The state of the body affects the way we look. When our health is compromised, it's reflected in our skin, our eyes, even our hair and nails. The state of the body can affect the relationships we have with others. When the state of your health is compromised, it is hard to be happy, and you won't have much love to give to others. This can kill any relationship you may have. What makes relationships grow is what you have to offer to others as a person, as a friend, as a mate, and as a lover.

The state of your body is directly linked to your self-esteem. When you don't look good physically, you may not feel good about yourself. Conversely, when you feel good about yourself physically, you feel good about who you are in general. Looking good physically doesn't have much to do with being toned; it has more to do with being at your best. I think it is important to embrace where you are physically now and always strive to be the best *you* that you can be.

Optimum health is what we should all strive for. It means that your body is in its best state health-wise. You wake up feeling refreshed every morning, you feel energized, and you have a stable good mood. In this state, the body has the capacity to heal faster, and it is able to bounce right back up after not feeling well. Your body is full of strength, and it is flexible.

Optimum health is something you achieve over time. In order to achieve this kind of health, you have to have daily rituals in place, a healthy mind-set, a deep sense of love for yourself, a deep appreciation for how your body works, and a commitment to be the best *you* that you can be. Anybody can achieve this level of health. The first step is believing that.

The relationship you have with your body and food is directly related to the way you feel about yourself and your life. When you don't love yourself, when you don't feel highly about yourself, and when you don't value yourself, you just won't care what you put in your body. You won't care how the things you do affect your body. You will most likely resort to a quick fix for a problem that took a while to develop to the state it's in. You won't listen to your body when it is telling you that something is wrong. In other words, when you don't love yourself, you neglect yourself and your body.

What is your relationship with your body and food? If the relationship is a negative one, I want you to consider your relationship with yourself. How do you feel about yourself? Do you love yourself?

Liking yourself is not enough. It is not deep enough, but love is. Love requires a certain level of passion that *like* lacks. When you love something, you take care of it with your life. When you love something, you make sure it is well taken care of; you don't leave it lying all over the place, and you make sure it is safe. You treat it like it is the most precious thing you own. When you like something, you don't treat it with the same passion.

Do you love yourself? If not, why not? What is it about yourself that makes you not love yourself? The way you feel about yourself is directly linked to the choices you make in food and the way you treat your body. It is important that you learn to see the value in you and know that you are a lovable person no matter how you look, what flaw you may have, what mistakes you have made in the past, or your ethnicity. You are a unique being. You were not designed to be like others, and you have so much to offer to others.

If you don't have a healthy, positive relationship with yourself, make this your priority now. This one change will have a domino effect on everything in your life. It will change the relationship that you have with your body and food.

How do you view your body? The way you view it affects your relationship with food. If you view your body as a precious temple to take great care of, your choices will reflect that. If you view your body as a living thing that gets hungry every few hours and you think you just have to be fine in order to do the things that you want to do, you won't care what you choose to eat. You will eat anything just to satisfy your hunger rather than because you want to nurture your body.

The view you have of your body is directly linked to your self-esteem. One of the things I believe helps change your view of your body for the better, besides loving yourself, is understanding how your body works. When you have an understanding of something, you can have an appreciation of it, because you are coming from a place of wisdom.

Know that your body is designed in a perfect way. Your body is designed to heal itself. Your body is designed to eliminate that which it doesn't need. Your body is designed to be in motion. Your body is designed to be energized. Yes, your body changes with time; yes, we do age. But this is not synonymous with chronic pain, constant and chronic inflammation, or disease.

Just like a car and a home need maintenance, just like they both need to be taken care of, so does your body. That maintenance and conditioning that your body needs, it gets through exercising several times a week, proper sleep, detoxification, and proper nutrition—not just of the body but of the mind and spirit as well. This means having the proper thoughts and emotions so that you can feel right about your body and the choices you make for it.

By "proper thoughts and emotions," I mean that you do your best to feel good about your life. You make the choice to feel hopeful and to expect goodness. You are thinking positive thoughts about yourself, you are thinking beautiful things about yourself, and you are thinking about how wonderful life is and can be.

I do not mean that you start imagining things that don't exist and that you do not have your feet on the ground. What I mean is that you remind yourself of all the goodness you still have in life. I believe that if you can see, if you can hear, if you can talk, and if you have your health, you already have everything. Even if you are missing some of those things, you still have so much good in your life. It's just a matter of taking a closer look at your life and seeing all the good you have.

When you are not happy with life, you are not thinking of eating healthy foods. Instead, your body craves foods that will pick you up emotionally, like sugar and simple carbohydrates. These are not

40

entirely bad, and you shouldn't avoid them completely—your body does need sugar and carbs. But your body will constantly crave these to make up for how you are feeling, and this is not good. Believe it or not, food is a drug, and like drugs, food does affect your mood.

Your mood determines to a certain extent what your body wants. This is why it is crucial that you are in control of your thoughts and emotions. When you control them, they don't control you. When you constantly eat sugary stuff and simple carbs, it is only a matter of time until your body starts giving up on you and no longer keeps your glucose level under control. This is how type 2 diabetes starts. A lot of diseases start because of our unhealthy lifestyle, and this is something that doesn't start overnight. These are habits you developed over time that perhaps you were not even aware of. It is important to remain aware of how you are feeling and thinking, because daily habits become our rituals, and we become what we do on a daily basis.

We are a product of what we did last year, last week, yesterday, and this morning. If you want your body to look and feel differently, you have to change your ways now. You have to make it your goal to take control of your thoughts and feelings. You have to make it your goal to change your unhealthy habits. You have to make it your goal to start loving yourself. You have to make it your goal to change your view of your body. You have to make it your goal to start listening to your body. You have to make it your goal to educate yourself about food and the body. You have to make the choice now. Every little thing that you do counts.

The way you treat your body in every way matters. It's never too late to change your ways and be a better person. Since everything creates a domino effect on your body and in life, you need to strive to feel good. One of the best ways is by feeding your soul. Feed it with healthy nutrients, such as positive thoughts and words. Feed it by watching beautiful and funny things. Feed it by listening to things that are uplifting. Feed it by surrounding yourself with positive people who love and accept you for who you are. When you feel good, you will want to continue doing things that make you feel good. You will start to choose foods that do your body good.

Every part of your body is in constant communication. Science has us believing that the different parts of our body are separate. If, for instance, you have arthritis, you see a rheumatologist. If you have depression, you see a psychiatrist. This gives the impression that there are two different things going on when in reality, there may be an underlying cause for both the arthritis and depression. This is why it is important to look at everything when it comes to your body, because your body is composed of so many things.

When one part of the body is affected, it is only a matter of time before another part or parts are affected as well. Blood cells are produced by bone marrow. The kidneys stimulate the production of bone marrow and help purify the blood. One can compare the blood to a transportation system, moving waste products, nutrients from the digestive system, and hormones. The skeleton is very connected to the muscular system, since muscles attach to bones. Muscle movement depends on the framework of the skeleton, and muscles need the right level of calcium in the blood in order to function properly.

Muscles also rely on the digestive system to get glucose for energy, and on the stimulation of the nerves for movement. The digestive system is important to the bones, since it supplies nutrients like phosphorus, glucosamine, and calcium. Did you know that estrogen plays a role in maintaining bone density, or that the endocrine system controls the balance of calcium? An imbalance in the level of calcium affects the heart and the muscles. If there is too much calcium, muscles can be over-relaxed, and if there is very little calcium, one can have muscle spasms.

I cannot stress enough how everything, every single part of us, is connected. This is why it is crucial for you to maintain your body and sustain it with nutritious foods. It is important that you care for every aspect of your life, since everything affects your body.

As a Wellness and Life Coach certified in both holistic nutrition and as a nutrition and wellness consultant, I've had the privilege of learning so much about the body. One of the things I somehow knew but confirmed through my learning is that your genes don't necessarily determine what disease you will suffer from. Ultimately, your lifestyle is the deciding factor. That is because through your lifestyle, you are sending messages to your genes, and they will respond accordingly. Your lifestyle includes your thoughts, your feelings, and your surroundings.

Don't allow your genes to condemn you to a life of type 2 diabetes, high cholesterol, high blood pressure, etc. You have great control over the state of your body through the choices you make on a daily basis. Everything you do is either nurturing your body or destroying it.

Your body was designed to work in perfect balance, but there are many things that can disrupt that balance, such as environmental toxins; toxins that are created within the body that don't get eliminated; lack of certain nutrients that your body needs; stress; lack of sleep; and lack of exercise. This is why it is important for you to take inventory of all that you do from the moment you wake up until the moment you go to sleep. Even your sleep affects the balance of your body. Don't ever take for granted any area of your life, not even sleep. Don't let yourself be fooled into thinking that one thing has nothing to do with the other. Look into your overall life on a consistent basis.

Start by creating a food journal and taking inventory of everything you eat for at least two weeks. The purpose of this journal is to make you pay attention to the foods you eat. If you're constantly feeling physically tired, you need to be aware of what you are putting in your body. Also, write down what mood you were in when you made that food choice. Pay attention to your habits and write them down. Our habits also influence our food choices.

Do you do a lot of social eating—that is, eat when you are in the company of others? Our social life does influence our choices of food. If you notice that when you are around your friends you tend to eat unhealthily, then choose other friends. When trying to make changes in life, you will notice that the people you surround yourself with will have to change as well. Writing everything down will help you see and know what you are doing that is leading you to the life you have now. If you want to understand how your body got to the state it's in, you have to see what you have been doing. Keeping a journal may sound boring, but I guarantee, it helps.

I want to encourage you to start viewing your body in a different way. View it as your temple and your true vehicle. Give it love no matter what state it is in. Appreciate your body even if you don't like the way it looks. Start by being grateful that you can move your body, that your body allows you to go to work, that you can still walk, that you can still move your arms, and that you can still achieve the goals you have. Even if you can't walk, if you can still move your arms, you still have things to be grateful for when it comes to your body. Be grateful that your body is still in good health. Whatever limitations you may have physically, remember all that you can still do thanks to your body.

If this isn't encouraging because you have a physical disability, become part of a group where there are people in your same situation with the same condition you have. This will help you see that you are not the only one going through what you are going through, and you will learn what others are doing to live a normal life. You will be surprised how inspiring it is to be surrounded by others with your same condition.

Make the most out of your body. It is beautiful just the way it is. It is the house of your true essence, which is your soul. Your soul is using your body as its vehicle in order to manifest its full expression. Therefore, start treating your body with respect.

I encourage you to learn more about your body. Watch webinars and read books on how the body works. If you have any physical illness, take the responsibility to learn about the illness and how you can heal your body. The more you learn, the better decisions you are able to make. Education is so valuable; understanding is what makes the difference in the choices we make. Don't limit yourself to just this one chapter. Go to the library or bookstore and learn much more. I promise you, it will change the way you view your body forever.

Start paying close attention to the messages your body is constantly giving you. Your body is always letting you know how something makes it feel. For example, feeling constantly tired may mean that your body is being overworked, it lacks sleep, it is very stressed, or it lacks nutrients. The things you think are minor may not be. If you constantly have headaches, pay attention to what you are eating or doing that may contribute to this. Don't be quick to take a painkiller, since that will only mask an underlying problem.

If a problem persists, by all means, go see your physician. Never wait until something is a big problem before you take notice of it. This is part of being mindful of the way you are living your life. It's a great way to take care of your body. Remember always that health starts with you.

Your body is the most precious thing you will ever own. It is unfortunate that many of us don't realize how precious our body is until we become sick. Your body to a great extent will determine the way you will live your life, and it affects the relationships you have with others. A healthy relationship with your body means you will make healthy choices. Do your best to educate yourself about your body. Pay attention to what it is telling you. Know what you are putting into your body and why. Do everything you can on a daily basis to give your body the proper maintenance. Start now to take care of your body, and you will see many dividends. I guarantee it.

## Things to Think About

- Your body is your precious home and vehicle.
- Take notice of how you feel about your body and yourself.
- Make sure you have a healthy relationship with your body.
- Take inventory of the foods you put in your body and what mood you were in when you made those choices.
- Educate yourself on how the body works.
- Understand that every part of the body is connected. When one part of your body is affected, it's only a matter of time before every other part is affected as well.
- Make a food journal for at least two weeks so that you can see what choices you are making and what changes you need to make.
- Pay attention to what your body is communicating to you on a daily basis.

# Value Your Sleep

Sleep is one of those things that we know so little about, and yet we cannot deny its importance. You can see and feel for yourself how important this is the moment you deprive yourself of sleep for one night. During the day, you may find it challenging to stay awake. It may be hard to concentrate. Your threshold level for irritation is much lower. Sleep plays a major role in every area of your life.

Some may consider sleep to be of not much importance, just something that robs us of time for doing other things. Some may even think that if they are tired or feel jet-lagged after a dramatic change in time zones, it is all in their mind. We live in a twenty-four-hour society constantly trying to delay and shorten our time for sleep, constantly disturbing the body's biological clock. It is no wonder we feel constantly sleep-deprived, frustrated, and hungry, craving high-calorie foods. If you feel any of the things I just mentioned, perhaps it's time to take a look at your sleep.

Sleep serves many functions that are medicinal to the body. This becomes very evident when we get sick, and all our body wants is bed. That's because sleep helps heal the body. The way to help both your brain and your body to be strong, alert, and productive is through sleep. When you don't get the amount of sleep your brain and body needs, your quality of life is affected.

Understanding sleep is essential to your well-being because sleep affects everything from your relationships to your ability to make decisions to your sense of hunger. Because everybody's body is different, your needs are going to be different, and this is also true when it comes to sleep. It is important for you to know how much sleep your body needs for you and your body to function at an optimum level. Because every now and then we do need to compromise our sleep, it's important to learn how you handle sleep deprivation.

Sleep experts recommend that you get adequate sleep in order to be mentally alert, energetic, in a good mood, and at your best. In order for you to value your sleep, it's important for you to understand what goes on while you are sleeping. While you are asleep, your brain is very active, carrying out many neurological, physiological, and biochemical tasks. These tasks are essential to your body's survival and the quality of your life. When you allow your body to sleep the amount of time that it needs, your brain and body can invigorate, renew, and repair itself. Sleep impacts so many aspects of your life: energy level, memory, body weight, hunger, threshold of anger and patience, and overall health. When you deny yourself sleep, your waking life is diminished significantly.

We live in a society where so much is demanded of us and sleep is not valued the way it should be. Yet we are biologically wired in such a way that we cannot function with little to no sleep. The price we pay for being sleep-deprived is too high. It includes low productivity at work, illnesses, accidents, and poor quality of life.

Physical changes occur when we sleep—in body temperature, heart rate, hormonal activity, brain waves, and muscle activity. Each stage of sleep plays a big role on our daytime life. It has an effect on the way the brain processes things, on our cardiovascular and gastrointestinal activity, and on our energy level.

Back in 1935, researchers at Harvard University realized that sleep has several stages that occur within an hour, from drowsiness to shallow sleep to deep sleep. Slow-wave sleep, which is also referred to as deep sleep, helps with restoration and growth. When we are in this deep sleep, muscles are getting more blood and restoration in the body is occurring. Those who exercise a lot or who have been sleep-deprived for a long period of time experience more deep sleep than usual.

During deep sleep, the body preserves energy by lowering its temperature. Tissue growth and repair take place at this time. The pituitary gland secretes growth hormones during this stage of sleep, stimulating the repair of body tissues, growth, and development. It is during this time that the immune system gets stronger. When you miss sleep, even if it's for one night, your body's capacity to fight viral infection is decreased. This is because interleukin and tumor necrosis factor, which are natural immune-system modulators in the body, are increased during deep sleep. Immune-system modulators are what help your body build resistance and fight disease.

I compare the immune-system to a country's military. Your immune system is your army, with the sole purpose of attacking anything that may hurt your body. It is your body's line of defense.

REM (rapid eye movement) sleep is the stage in which people start having dreams. This stage is known for its eye movement, and this is when the brain is very active. The sympathetic nervous system is more active during this phase of sleep than when the body is awake. There is more blood flowing to the brain. Blood pressure, breathing, and pulse increase, as well as body temperature. This is when men tend to experience an erection and women experience lubrication and vaginal swelling. You do not need to have a sexual dream for this to occur. It occurs naturally, and the reason is still not clear, according to experts.

During REM sleep, the eyes begin to dart back and forth.

The neuronal messages that are sent from the motor cortex of the brain are blocked at the brain stem. Because of this, your muscles are completely relaxed, and you don't move. This is a good thing, because otherwise we all would be acting out our dreams. When the part of the brain responsible for blocking the messages sent from the motor cortex is impaired, you are able to move your body even though you are asleep.

REM sleep aids your ability to store, retain, and organize memories and learn new things. The brain is busy firing neurons, which is what is believed to be responsible for the storage of memory and the organizing and classifying of information. When something new is learned or experienced, certain neurons form in the brain that make specific connections with other neurons. This creates a chain of neurons called neural networks or memory traces that are spread throughout the brain. This is where memory is stored. REM sleep is what helps these neural connections grow. In essence, REM sleep stimulates the brain to retain the memories we create and store them in the long-term memory part of the brain. Without REM sleep, your memory is impaired.

The neurotransmitters norepinephrine and serotonin are believed to play a role in the ability to learn and retain new information. Neurotransmitters help neurons to communicate with other neurons. During your waking time, these two neurotransmitters are used up. They are replenished while you are in REM sleep. Obviously, then, REM sleep is essential for your ability to learn and retain new information.

How do you know you are sleep deprived? Indicators include the following:

- drowsiness during the day

- micro sleeps, which are short moments of sleep that last a few seconds at a time
- changes in mood, including depression, irritability, and loss of sense of humor
- weight gain
- feeling cold (this is because when you stay up very late at night, the biological clock causes your body temperature to drop)
- decreased immunity
- loss of motivation
- inability to concentrate
- inability to remember
- inability to analyze new information

Often we don't realize these symptoms because we have become accustomed to thinking that it is normal to not have much energy or to feel tired. It is not. You are indeed meant to feel energized, but you have to help your body feel this way. One way is through getting enough quality sleep.

The homeostatic sleep drive basically has the job of making sure we get the amount of sleep we need so that we can remain awake during the day. This continues to work even while we are awake, because as we remain awake, the need for sleep starts to build. The biological clock, also called circadian rhythm, is made up of two small neural structures found in the center of the brain. Circadian rhythm controls body temperature, level of alertness, and hormone production. For those who may be curious as to what *circadian* means, it comes from the Latin word "around the day." *Circa* means "around" and *dies* meaning "a day." Your circadian rhythm is influenced by your exposure to light. When you expose yourself to light, this signals the brain not to secrete melatonin, which is a hormone that signals your body to sleep.

Despite the fact that the circadian rhythm is affected by light, it still works without exposure to light. In 1985, Dr. Dale Edgar studied monkeys while they were in an environment of constant dim light and constant temperature—basically an environment that wasn't changing. What he noticed was that the monkeys behaved as if they were exposed to a daylight schedule where the sun rose and set. The monkeys were awake for fifteen to sixteen hours and would go to sleep for eight or nine hours. This helped researchers reach the conclusion that indeed there is an internal clock controlling our sleeping and waking cycles.

This explains why even if you are exposed to light because you are in a foreign country with, say, a six-hour time difference, you can still feel sleepy. You biological clock has not yet adjusted to the big time change. Sleep experts in this case suggest that we maintain our biological clock in synchrony with our daily routine. That way, we sleep when we are supposed to sleep and stay awake when we are supposed to stay awake.

Sleep experts have several suggestions of changes to make to improve your sleep. They include the following:

- Decrease your caffeine intake. Experts recommend avoiding anything with caffeine—such as tea, coffee, or soda—within six hours of your bedtime. Caffeine is a stimulant that can delay your sleep and disturb your REM sleep. Experts also recommend that you avoid foods high in sugar as well as chocolate, since chocolate also has caffeine.

- Associate your bed with sleep and relaxation. When in bed, use that time to either sleep or have sex and nothing else.

- Right before bed, do things that are relaxing to you instead of stimulating. You can read a good book, but beware that lights disturb your sleep, since it can prevent your brain from secreting the melatonin that signals your body to sleep. You can listen to music that relaxes you or do yoga. The point is that you want to do something that takes your mind away from the worries of the day and gets you ready for sleep.

- Do not smoke. Nicotine stimulates brain wave activity and raises your blood pressure and heart rate. This will not help you sleep or remain asleep.

- Eat a healthy diet. Do your best to avoid foods that cause indigestion or that raise your glucose level very high. When you eat foods that raise your glucose level, your body secretes large amounts of insulin, which contributes to fat storage. This increases the likelihood of indigestion.

- Do your best to lower your stress levels. Stress doesn't have to be a bad thing. If we are to look at the positive aspects of stress, it fuels us to want to get things done or to stay away from a situation that is not conducive to our health. Because there are times that the stress of life doesn't allow us to sleep, it is important to learn how to manage stress. Breathing deeply and exhaling out for a couple of minutes helps. Find things that relax you, and make sure to keep things in perspective. Exercising also helps with your stress levels, since it causes the brain to secrete endorphins and serotonin, which help us feel good.

- Stop trying so hard to go to sleep. This kind of pressure actually hinders you from falling asleep. If for some reason you have trouble sleeping, either do something that relaxes you or get out of bed and just sit or stand. Avoid turning on the light, since light can further hinder you from falling asleep.

- If you have tried different things to go to sleep and nothing works, go to a sleep specialist. Get a referral from your doctor or do some research.

There are times when we can't fall asleep because the bedroom is not a positive sleeping environment. There are many things that influence this. One of them is room temperature. Now, everybody's body is different, and because of this everybody's needs will be different. However, in general, the room temperature that is suitable for most is between 62 and 70 degrees Fahrenheit. A very cold or very hot room can be very disruptive to sleep.

The amount of light in a room also affects sleep. Remember, light signals the brain to stop the release of melatonin, which helps signal the body to go to sleep. If the room isn't dark enough for you, consider wearing an eyeshade.

A very noisy room can disturb sleep. There are noises that rather than being calming are stimulating, and this doesn't help you go to sleep. If for some reason there is too much noise and it disturbs your sleep, you can get a white-noise generator, which will help block out the noises that are disrupting your sleep.

Consider whether or not your room is clean and in order. This too can affect your sleep. A very messy room adds to your stress level, preventing you from falling asleep. The colors in a room also affect the way you feel, so select colors that are relaxing to you. Consider also what you are wearing to go to sleep. There are some pajamas that make you itch or feel hot. This too can disturb your sleep.

Your bed also plays a role in how well you sleep. How is your mattress? Make sure that you choose the mattress that is right for you. When shopping for a mattress, the Better Sleep Council recommends you use the S.L.E.E.P. test. S.L.E.E.P. stands for the following steps:

- Select a mattress.
- Lie down on your typical sleep position.
- Evaluate the level of comfort and support.
- Educate yourself about each selection.
- Partners should test beds together.

The Better Sleep Council suggests that you research different types and sizes of mattresses before you shop for one. If you can't decide which one to buy, think of a time when you either stayed at a hotel or someone's house and had a good night's sleep. Start from there to determine the right mattress for you.

When you go to the store, ask a knowledgeable salesperson to help you purchase the right mattress for you. When you are in the store, "test-drive" the mattress. Lie on the bed for a few minutes and close your eyes so you can know how you feel on the mattress. Try different kinds of mattresses and lie on them in the same position you are in when you sleep. Give yourself up to fifteen minutes to relax on the mattress so you can truly get a feel for it.

Moving on from mattresses, how is your pillow? The wrong pillow can disturb your sleep. If your pillow doesn't adjust to your neck and head, it is time to get a new one. Dr. James B. Maas, author of *Power Sleep: The Revolutionary Program That Prepares Your Mind for Peak Performance*, suggests that you test your pillow for support. Do this by folding the pillow in half and letting it go. A pillow with support will unfold and return to its original shape.

One thing I cannot leave out of this chapter is jet lag. As part of the inflight airline industry, I know very well what jet lag can do to one's well-being and body, and how important it is to learn how to manage jet lag—that is, the interruption of the body's biological clock caused by crossing multiple time zones very quickly. There are several symptoms of jet lag, including delayed reaction time, feeling disoriented, inability to concentrate, sleepiness during the day, difficulty sleeping at night, gastrointestinal problems, and irritability.

According to Dr. Maas, there are several things you can do to combat jet lag. The list is really long, so I will include only those I can't leave out:

- Do your best not to lose any sleep before your trip. This is why experts recommend that you try not to choose a flight that leaves very early, just to avoid missing sleep. That way you don't have a sleep debt when you arrive at your destination.

- If you only plan on staying a day or two at a new destination with a big time difference, try not to reset your biological clock to the new time, since you will then have to reset it again when you go back home.

- If you're going to a destination with a big time difference for business purposes, try to schedule your meeting at a time where you are still alert. That may be late afternoon or evening at the country you're going to. The point is to schedule the meeting at a time when your biological clock is in an alert state.

- Do your best to be calm when preparing for a trip. This means preparing things ahead of time.

- While in flight, drink lots of water in order to stay hydrated. Dehydration can delay the process of adjusting your biological clock to that of the destination time.

- While in flight, avoid drinking alcohol, since alcohol can accelerate dehydration and impede the body's capacity to process oxygen.
- While in flight, eat and sleep as if you were already at your destination's time zone.
- Light can help you adjust your biological clock to the destination time, so use the daylight to help with this.
- For those in the inflight service industry, I recommend using cocoons. These look like sunglasses, but they are not. They can be worn on top of your own eyeglasses. What they do is block the blue light that is emitted from both lightbulbs and sunlight. Wear these when you step off the plane. That encourages your brain to release melatonin, which will help you fall asleep when you arrive at the hotel.

I also highly recommend that you eat a healthy diet, one that is right for your body. Since everybody's body is different, your needs will be different from everyone else. For instance, I'm allergic to dairy. After I either eat or drink dairy, I have headaches that go all the way to my eyeballs and I also start getting congested—all of which makes sleep difficult. A healthy diet for me consists of no dairy. Yours will be personal to you. When you eat a healthy diet, your body is able to bounce back quickly from things like jet lag, as opposed to when you eat junk food. Food is your body's fuel. It is equivalent to putting gasoline in your car.

Sleep is so important to your overall well-being that it has to be an area of your life that you look into and pay attention to if you want to improve your life overall. If you constantly feel hungry, tired, irritable, short of energy, or very stressed, I urge you to look into this area of your life. Contact a sleep specialist if necessary. Ignoring this area of your life is truly doing a disservice to yourself. The price you pay is very high.

Start now to implement better sleep habits. Start now to look into the foods you eat that are influencing your sleep. Start now to create a bedroom that is conducive to a good night's sleep. Start now to take inventory of this area of your life.

## Things to Think About

- Sleep is a crucial part of your overall well-being.
- It affects every area of your life, from your appetite to your relationships to your productivity.
- If you constantly feel tired, hungry, and lacking in motivation, consider how you are sleeping.
- There are many factors that influence your sleep, from what you do right before bed to the foods you eat, your sleep habits, and even your bed itself.
- If you have tried everything and nothing works, contact a sleep specialist.

# Set Your Mind Right

One of the things that has to be right before anything can be right in your life is your mind. Your actions, emotions, every decision you make, the words you speak, the way you react to things, your perspective—all of these start in the mind. The right mind-set is everything. Without this, nothing can fall into place. Before you can understand that you deserve a life full of health, clarity, happiness, love, and energy, your mind must be right. Setting your mind right is critical to creating the life you want and deserve.

No person, no circumstance, no thing can give you the life you want. Only you can do that, by setting your mind right. This needs to be a priority for you. You will be creating the mental, emotional, and spiritual agility necessary to deal with the everyday things of life. When your mind is right, you emit a high degree of positive energy that will attract to you the things that you want. There is no way you can do this when mentally you are focusing on all the wrong things.

There are great consequences to focusing on all the wrong things. Your emotions follow your mind, and your body follows your emotions. Your thoughts affect the way you feel, and how you feel affects your body. If you want to feel energetic, you have to be mindful of how you feel; if you want to feel happy, you have to be mindful of your thoughts. Your thoughts are energy. Your thoughts are magnets attracting what you think about. When you focus on the wrong things, all you can see is negative. Focusing on the negative steals your joy, your ability to think straight, and your ability to see the good. It robs you of your good health. When you don't set your mind right, you can't get clarity. It's as if your mind is cloudy—and indeed it is! How can you think with clarity when your mind is in the wrong place?

How do you know when your mind is in the wrong place? When you think a lot about the past, when you think too much about your regrets, when you place too much of your attention on someone or something other than yourself, when you're so concerned about what others will think, when you're seeking other people's approval … the list goes on and on. You will know when your mind is in the wrong place because it will manifest in your everyday living. Your feelings are indicators of where your thoughts are. It will seem as if everything is going wrong; how can it not when that is your focus?

To see and feel changes in your life, shift your mind-set and the way you feel. This is going to be different for everybody, so do what works for you. Setting your mind-set straight doesn't have to be complicated. You don't have to travel far to get that mental shift.

I believe that one of the best and longest-lasting ways to get that mental shift is by listening to your soul, which is your true essence. When you listen to your true essence, you are being your true self, and there is nothing like being your true self. There is a sense of happiness that comes with being your true self. Your self-esteem rises when you listen to yourself, because you start to gain confidence. You start gaining a real understanding of who you truly are, and understanding who you are is powerful.

You do this by reminding yourself that you are in control of your thoughts. You control how something is going to make you feel. Find something to think about that makes you feel good so you can think of that whenever you feel bad. Pick something to focus on so that you are not paying attention to minor details. When you have a bigger picture to focus on, it will give you the strength to keep moving forward, even when the going gets tough.

Your mind-set is everything. Before you did something, it was first in your mind. You first thought about it, and then you acted. What you think about affects your emotions. Because your actions are influenced by what you think and feel, you need to be aware of your thoughts. When your mind is right, this is when you are able to get things done. You have the capacity to tolerate things you didn't think you could. You have the mental, emotional, and physical endurance to handle things you would not have otherwise. Your life stems from your mind-set.

When your mind is all over the place, you feel as if you don't have the strength to deal with things. Your behavior isn't consistent, because it reflects what you think and feel, and this changes from time to time. You have to do with your mind what you would with your pet: take control over it. Don't just let it do whatever it wants to do; it may not be pretty.

In order to set your mind right, you need clarity about what you want out of life. This helps you determine what you need to do to get what you want. You may notice that although you have clarity about certain things in life, there are other issues that keep you from the life you want—fear or laziness, to name two. It is important to deal with these issues and figure out where they are coming from.

If fear is keeping you from what you want, ask yourself what you are afraid of. Is it failure? What makes you think you are going to fail? Is it a lack of knowledge? Work on acquiring the knowledge you need. Is it a lack of confidence? Question that. You want to fully understand what is stopping you from having the mind-set you need to achieve your goals.

Another way to get your mind-set right is by establishing healthy habits. These habits consist of sleeping right, eating right, being physically active, feeding both your mind and spirit with positive stuff, and surrounding yourself with loving people. This may sound repetitive, but it's because one thing does affect the other.

Sleep very much affects your thinking, your ability to retain information, and your personality. What you eat also affects your thinking, because every cell of your body is fed by what you put in your body. A lack of nutritious foods can keep your mind from functioning at an optimum level. Exercising helps release certain feel-good hormones that are crucial to your happiness, and as the saying goes, "A body in motion stays in motion." When you are working out, you are much more likely to get more done. Exercising helps with your blood circulation, it helps with your mood, it helps build muscle, and it gives you a sense of accomplishment to know that you are taking care of yourself.

A good workout doesn't necessarily mean hitting the gym for two hours. Just ten minutes at home can suffice if you are just starting out. The point is that you want to start getting in some type of physical activity. Acquiring a habit takes time. Keep at it.

Another way to set your mind right is by knowing your priorities. Write down on a sheet of paper what is most important to you at the moment. List the things you want to achieve in the short and long term. There is something about knowing your priorities that helps you to be in alignment with what you want. When you don't know what your priorities are or what you want, you will be all over the place, and you don't want to be all over the place. Knowing your priorities helps keep you organized and focused so that you can start living a purposeful life.

## Things to Think About

- Your mind-set is key to a balanced and happy life.
- Everything in your life stems from your mind-set.
- No person, no thing, and no circumstance can give you the life you want. You are the only person who can do this, and you do it by setting your mind right.
- Establish healthy habits.
- Shift your focus to the right things.
- Take control of your mind.

# Choose Work That You Love

Obviously, there are many things that influence your well-being. Some of them are more obvious than others, but one that definitely and heavily influences your well-being in every way and that creates a ripple effect in every other area of your life is the work you choose to do. This is a very important area to look into, because your work influences your thoughts, your presence in life, and the way you present yourself to your family after you come back from work. It influences your energy levels and the way you feel about yourself.

This goes more for men than women, because a lot of a man's identity is wrapped up in the work he does. That's just the reality of it. Women tend to value the relationships we have with other people more than the work we do. Work is still important, though, and it does form some part of our identity if we're not careful.

It is very important to know how to separate your identity from the work you do. It can be very unhealthy to identify yourself only with your work. Don't let the job you do define you. You are much more than that. But the reality is that the work we do does impact the way we feel about ourselves. If you don't pay attention to this area, you're ignoring something huge that is impacting you in every way on a daily basis.

For some of you, at the present time, it may feel like you have no choice about the work you do. You have responsibilities like paying the bills, paying the rent, and sustaining a family, so it feels like any job will do. However, it is very important to pay attention, because choosing a job that you enjoy is fundamental to your well-being in every regard. When you choose a job you love and enjoy, you will feel happier when you get back home to your family.

I'm not saying that a job you love will not have challenges and stress. Every job has its down moments, every single one. But the challenges won't seem so gigantic in comparison to those of a job you do not like. A job you do not like is almost like putting poison in your soul; it will slowly kill you. This is because you will feel miserable waking up in the morning knowing that you have to go to a place you do not want to go. Forcing yourself to have the energy to go and do the things you do not want to do is just plain negative for you. Whether it's the environment you don't like or the people you work with, that is a miserable state of being. It affects your energy levels, your mental health, your emotional health, and your thought process. If what you do doesn't make you feel good, then you are not doing what you were meant to be doing.

Doing a job that you do not want to do robs you of your presence in life. It keeps you from being present in the moment. How so? You do not want to be there physically or mentally, so your mind may wander around. You are trying to take a mental vacation because it's the only way for you to survive the days and the hours that you have to spend at that job.

We spend the majority of our time at work, so it's only fair that you choose a job you enjoy and can get something out of. It is by being present in the moment that you are going to feel that you are in a flow. There is no way you can feel flow if you are doing a job you do not like. Been there, done that, and I know it feels miserable.

It's especially miserable if you have a family to go home to, and your kids have to see parents who hate their work life. What are you teaching your kids? At every moment, you are a role model, and you are sending messages that they internalize as belief. Kids mimic what we do. This is not the message that you want to give to your kids.

If you're a man reading this, know that your wife needs you to come back home with some energy to be present as a husband and father. Your wife needs you to still be loving. How can you be loving when you hate what you do on a daily basis? When you feel like you do not have enough for yourself because you are so exhausted when you come from work, you certainly do not have enough to give to others. When you feel like your job sucks the life out of you, you do not have anything to give, so whatever little bit you have, you want to keep to yourself because you need it for you. This is no way to be. The way to remedy this is by choosing a job that you love.

How do you choose work you love? I'm going to seem like a broken record, but I seriously mean it, and there is no way around it: you need to know yourself. Unless you know who you are, what you like, what you can and can't tolerate, what you are capable of doing, what your limitations are, what you expect from an employer, what you expect from yourself, what your skills are, and what you still have to learn, you will not know what job you can do. You need to take the time to get to know these things about yourself.

So take the time, have a journal if you must, but write down your skills, your level of education, and your hobbies. Write down the things you enjoy doing and learning. All these things are indicators of the kind of job you can see yourself doing.

Once you know these things about yourself, take the time to research jobs or careers that require the skills you already have. Do that research. If anything intrigues you, do more research and see what the job entails. Learn what is expected of you from that kind of job and what the employer requires of you for the interview. The point is, you want to do as much digging and research about yourself and what is out there as you can. You will be surprised to learn that there are jobs perfectly aligned to who you are. What you are meant to be doing is out there waiting for you.

Choosing a job that matches who you are, with the help of the research you've done, will bring you into alignment. It's going to help you feel more joy in life. It's going to help you achieve some of the dreams and goals that you have. It will add more health to your life, because you will feel that life has more meaning to you.

It is important for your mental and emotional health to feel that your life is meaningful. This is why I encourage you to think about your goals and see if the job you are considering helps you reach them. For instance, if your goal is to be in a position of leadership, look for a job that provides an opportunity for growth. Know that no job is perfect; that's not what you're looking for. You're looking for a job that matches your true essence so that you can be happy and healthy in life.

Every day should be an opportunity to be achieving something, even if it is something small. Allow this to happen. You want to make sure that every day you are making yourself happy, because by being happy, you are making yourself healthy. If you're currently frustrated, you may not even realize that it's because of the work you do. It's essential to look into this part of your life.

There are always choices. If for whatever reason you have to stay where you are, choose to change your perspective. No matter what it is you're doing, no matter the circumstance you are in, you can always get something out of it, whether a learning experience or a new resource that is going to make you into a better person. You have to be willing to look for the learning experience.

Try to figure out what it is about the job that you don't like. This is a positive thing to know, because in order to find a job you will love, you need to know what you hate. Part of understanding yourself is knowing what you dislike and why. This is going to give you a clue as to who you are.

For example, I know I am not an office person. I've done office jobs, and I know I do not like them. I'm more of a creative person and a people person. In my opinion, there is nothing creative about being in an office. I'm a bird, and I like to fly. That represents freedom to me. I like the possibility of growth, and to me there is no growth in being in an office. I'm pretty sure that for some people, there is growth there, and that is great for them. But because of my nature and my soul, that is not healthy for me. Being in an office goes against who I am.

Even if you dislike a job, you are probably gaining some skills. Think about what those may be. You are always learning something, no matter how small it may be. Probably you're learning how to use a computer or certain applications. You may be learning organizational skills, interpersonal skills, patience—whatever it is, there is something you are learning. Maybe it's what not to do in a job interview or how to communicate better. There's always something to draw from every job you have.

Try to squeeze all the resources from that job you dislike. I'm not talking about physical resources; I'm not a believer in using your job for personal gain. This is cheating and robbing from the company that offered you a job. I'm referring to things you can learn that will help you be a better person for the next job and make a better choice. You are going to need references. Make sure that even though you don't like what you're doing, you don't burn any bridges and compromise the chance of getting a good reference letter.

Even at a job you don't like, you can meet beautiful people with whom, after that job, you can have a beautiful friendship. There was one office temporary job I did where I met a wonderful friend, and we have been friends now for more than eight years. How beautiful is that! Remember, there is something positive to be found in anything.

One thing I want to put out there that I think will be helpful—especially if you are doing a job that you do not like and you do not have a family to take care of —is to use some of the money you make to explore, learn, grow, and investigate other options that are out there. Educate yourself with new skills, a certification, perhaps even a degree. Start your own business as a way to have another income. We are living in a time where unfortunately no job is secure, so if you can start your own business, you can give yourself employment. You can be your own asset. I think it's a great way to never be without a job.

Making a right choice about your work life is something you will not regret. It may be a challenge at first, and it may feel like the job you want is too grand, but in this wonderful world, nothing is too grand. The sky truly is the limit. If you propose this to yourself and put the intention out there and take action, you will find that job. Things have a way of showing up and coming to you if you are willing to believe. I encourage you to take the steps necessary to have the job that you deserve.

## Things to Think About

- Choosing a job that you enjoy is essential to your well-being.
- Your job influences your thoughts, your presence in life, the way you present yourself to your family after you come back from work, your energy levels, and even the way you may feel about yourself.
- Doing a job you despise is like putting poison in your soul.
- In order for you to choose a job that you want and that is right for you, you need to know yourself.

- Do the research to learn all that is out there regarding the things that you like.
- If you can't change the job you currently have for whatever reason, change your perspective.
- Squeeze out of the experience all that you can for your growth.

# Start Your Morning Right

Your morning sets the tone for the rest of the day. Notice that when you wake up "on the wrong side of the bed," it seems like your whole day goes wrong. This is because what you do in the morning creates a domino effect that carries on throughout the day. That's how important it is to start your morning right.

For example, if you wake up feeling sad or dread the day ahead, these very feelings and thoughts make you think negative things, which draws negative things to you. If something good happens but you're feeling negative, your negative feelings and thoughts overshadow the good. You cannot afford to do that to yourself! You may not feel it right away, but all this will eventually make you physically sick. All these negative thoughts and feelings put unnecessary stress on your body. If you want to live a vibrant and energetic life, you cannot afford to put unnecessary stress on yourself.

Even if you are reading this midday or at night, you can start right now to set your morning right. Think positive, beautiful thoughts before going to bed. I personally don't like watching the news at night and so I don't, and I've noticed a difference. When I used to watch the news at night, watching all the bad things occurring in the world depressed me, and I didn't realize it until I noticed that I would wake up most of the time feeling negative about the world. This might not be true for you, but I believe that

71

what you speak, see, or hear right before bed has an effect on how you feel in the morning. If you watch TV before bed, I recommend watching something funny, relaxing, or inspiring. Watch things that are positive for your mind and your soul.

Don't go to bed angry or sad. These emotions tend to carry throughout the morning. This is when it is important to communicate your emotions so that you don't hold them in but communicate in a way that will lead to further understanding and to getting the results you want. If it is a situation that made you angry, think about the lessons from that experience. There is always something to learn every single day, and from every situation and person. Try to see what the lessons are and vow to yourself to be a better person as a result of what happened.

If something bad happened that makes you feel bad—such as grieving a loved one or the end of a relationship—give yourself time to grieve by setting some sad time aside for yourself. Someone told me this once, and although it may sound kind of ridiculous, it does work. Set aside time to cry over whatever it is that makes you cry, but once that time is over, that's it. You dry your tears and move on.

It is necessary to feel grief. Pushing that aside and acting like what happened didn't affect you leads to more hurt in the long run. It is like having a big deep wound and, instead of giving it the proper attention and care that it needs and giving it time to fully heal, you act like it's not there by placing a bandage over it. The wound is still there, hurting and not healing at all. The best way to grieve is by going through the emotions. It is not easy, but in the long run, you do heal over time, to the point that you just see a scar instead of a wound.

I think the morning is the best time to thank life, God, the universe, or whatever it is you believe in for giving you another day. It is the time to feel gratitude for life. It is the time to look

72

forward to the day ahead in a positive way. The morning is the best time for you to imagine how great the day is going to be. Expect that your day is going to be great, good things are going to come, and beautiful surprises await you. That sense of expectancy starts drawing things to you. Imagine and believe that you are going to get a lot accomplished.

The morning is a new beginning. It's a fresh new day and a time for renewal. It's a chance to be a better version of yourself. It's an opportunity for more wisdom. The more you start viewing your mornings in a new, positive light, the brighter your day will be.

Make sure you wake up early enough that you have time to do all the things you have to do without rushing. I don't know about you, but when I rush in the morning, it puts me in a bad mood. It changes the state of my body in a bad way, and it just sets the wrong tone for the day. You want to make sure you are centered, and being in a rush takes you out of your center. Being centered is what will allow you to be balanced and to bounce back when things get thrown in your way.

For those who may not understand what being centered means, it is a state of calm, inner peace, and connection with yourself. You are one with yourself. This requires stillness. When you are centered, you are able to endure things better than when you are not centered. Learning to do this is an art that takes time to master, but once you do, you will feel you can manage things with a bit more ease.

I would also suggest that either the night before or first thing in the morning, you make a list of the things you would like to accomplish during the day. This sets the tone for the day, gives you a sense of purpose, and helps you accomplish more. It sets your mind right as well, because you are putting things in order of priority. Everything you do is connected to everything else. Setting your mind right will set your morning right, and vice versa. You can't really separate one thing from another; they all work together to balance things out.

Setting your morning right is also part of creating a lifetime of well-being, because if you want your day to go right, you need to set the right tone from the start. You do that in the morning. When your morning is set right, it almost feels as if everything starts to happen with ease.

## Things to Think About

- The morning sets the tone for the day.
- Before going to bed, either watch, talk about, or listen to beautiful things.
- Don't go to bed sad or angry. These emotions tend to carry throughout the morning.
- The morning is the best time to thank God, the universe, or life for another day. This sense of gratefulness can attract more goodness into your life.
- The morning is a new beginning, another opportunity to be a better version of yourself.
- Wake up early so that you have enough time to do the things you have to do without rushing.
- The tone in the morning determines how centered you will be throughout the day.
- Make a list the night before or in the morning of the things you want to accomplish that day.

# Make Yourself Responsible for Your Life

Your life is your responsibility. Your happiness is your responsibility. Your health is your responsibility. Your mental, emotional, and spiritual states are your responsibility. As long as you are placing these responsibilities on someone else, you will never be happy. You will never have the life you want. You will never be the person you were meant to be.

The moment you become an adult, all these responsibilities fall on you. No longer are your parents responsible for your life, for what you do, or for what you are capable of doing. If there were or are any issues as a result of your upbringing, it's now your responsibility to resolve them.

The problem with blaming your parents or relatives for the life you have now is that you will continue with the same issues you currently have. You are making yourself a victim of your past. This way of thinking doesn't allow you to see your role in how you can overcome the issue at hand. Seeing yourself as a victim means you have no role in what happened and no fault, and there is nothing you can do about it.

I would like to clarify that I am not implying that whatever happened to you during childhood is your fault. Not at all! As children, we are innocent. We didn't ask to be born. I am merely suggesting that as an adult, you can make a conscious choice not to allow your childhood issues to hinder your greatness. You have a choice to grow from your experiences, and placing yourself in the victim position keeps you from doing that.

You are responsible for having the life you want. Nobody can give you what you're looking for; you need to give it to yourself. If you don't do your part, it doesn't matter how much others support you or are there for you. You are the one who needs to put in the effort.

Make yourself responsible for your life by knowing and fully believing that no one can actually make you feel any particular way. Only you can make yourself feel what you feel. Take control of your mind, thoughts, and actions. I learned this the hard way, and I am still learning that if I can master my thoughts and my mind, I can be a master of my life.

We are emotional beings, and as such many of the decisions we make are based on our emotions. Life consists of many small decisions that we make on a daily basis. You want to make sure that you are feeling good emotionally and making the right choices. We tend to manifest what we think and feel, so mastering your thoughts is crucial.

You master your mind by challenging any limiting beliefs you may have. When you don't challenge your limiting beliefs, you allow that invisible glass ceiling to exist that is preventing you from being and achieving your best. You may be surprised to learn that perhaps some of the limiting beliefs you have are actually other people's beliefs that were placed in you until you actually owned the belief. Perhaps it is a belief that was created as a result of something that happened to you.

Whatever the reason for the belief, it is important to confront it, question it, challenge it, and change it. This is something that takes time. You will experience resistance, but I encourage you to continue challenging that belief. The person you want to be and the life you want to live are right behind that resistance. The resistance means that something within you is changing for the better.

When you start to work out and have either never worked out before or haven't worked out in a long time, you feel sore after the workout. Just because you are sore doesn't mean that the workout doesn't work; it just means that you are working muscles you have never used before. Resistance is equivalent to that soreness. You are working muscles you haven't used before. There are changes taking place as a result of challenging your limiting beliefs.

Take responsibility for your health by ensuring that you care for your body the way it is meant to be taken care of. Make sure to eat right by fueling your body. Do your best to incorporate physical activity into your life. Know what medications you take and the side effects. Make sure to get the amount of sleep your body needs. Don't leave the responsibility for your health to your doctor. That is wrong and not fair for you. No one will care more about your body than you. No one can really take care of your body the way you can. To learn more about how to take care of your body, read the "Nurture Your Body" chapter in this book.

You can take responsibility for your emotional health in many ways. Allow only healthy, fulfilling relationships in your life. It's easy to take for granted how important the relationships that we have in our life are to our overall health. Do your best to see the positive side of things. This can be a challenge at times, but we must realize that our perception of things greatly influences the way we feel about them. Establish positive goals for yourself.

Setting positive goals gives you something to look forward to and strive for. Part of waking up feeling good about life is having something to look forward to, and working toward goals does just that. Make time to listen to your true self. Doing this provides you with answers and tools you didn't even know you had.

Your true self will guide you to happiness. Allow yourself to become a genuine giver; give truly without expecting anything in return. There is something about genuinely giving to others that makes us feel good, plus you give off positive energy that you get right back, and this adds to your emotional health. You ensure that you do things that make you happy; that's what makes life worth living.

Do your best to diminish the amount of stress in your life. I don't think stress was meant to be absent from our lives, since it does serve a purpose. Stress is what prepares us for a "fight or flight" response to dangerous situations. The problem comes when we allow stress to be a constant companion. Stress should be reserved for real emergencies.

When we allow unnecessary stress into our life, we compromise our overall well-being, from our emotional state to our physical state. Anything that isn't an emergency and places you in a constant state of stress is not worth it. The illnesses you can get as a result of constant stress are numerous. It can range from high blood pressure to even accelerating the growth of cancer cells. You can avoid this by understanding what triggers stress for you and finding ways to decrease your levels of stress.

There are several ways you can lower your stress. One that I highly recommend—if you are currently facing challenging moments in your life that causes you stress—is reaching out to those who love you and who you trust. Keeping things bottled up is no good for you. Every little thing that happens adds up to the point that you feel like you can't take it anymore. Reaching out to others is a sign of strength. It takes courage to know when you need help and support.

78

Another way to decrease your stress level is by doing things that relax you—anything from meditation, yoga, and working out to watching a comedy or reading a book. Find what works for you and take some time every day to do that activity. Relaxing is not a luxury. It is a necessity, especially in today's world that requires so much of us. The more responsibilities you have and the more you do, the more you need to relax. What relaxing does is help you recharge your batteries so that you will have the energy to do what you must do.

Sometimes our thoughts are stressful. If you don't have control of them, they can run free and do whatever they want. One way to overcome this is to be aware of your thoughts and understand why you are having those thoughts to begin with. Challenge your thoughts and do your best not to allow them to control you. A change in perspective can do wonders if you allow it.

If it's a person who is stressing you, know that you have a choice to either minimize the amount of contact you have with that person or stay away from that person altogether. You don't need people in your personal space who stress you. It's not worth it. Life is too short and beautiful for that.

Avoid people who drain you if you can. Otherwise, minimize your time with them. Only have contact when necessary. If you need to get along because of work, do the specific job you have to do and that's it. If it's a relative, do your best to just be in touch when necessary. This is all part of you taking responsibility for your life.

Take responsibility for the mistakes you made. When you avoid doing so, you never draw the lessons that are waiting for you there. Blaming others for your faults is useless for you. Perhaps the other person was somewhat at fault, but you also played a role in what happened. When you can admit to your own faults, you open yourself up to being a better person. Strive to be a better you every day. Do your best to grow from every experience, even from your mistakes. It will serve you well, plus when another similar situation occurs, you will know how to react.

Take responsibility for the choices you make. Every day you are making small decisions that add up to who you are today and all that you will be tomorrow. Whether you realize it or not, every decision that you make, no matter how small, either adds to or takes away from your health. When you choose to eat junk food, you are taking away from your health. When you choose to be angry, you are taking away from your health. When you choose to have negative thoughts, you are taking away from your health. Even not doing anything about anything is a choice.

Everything is an investment, and there are so many ways in which you are investing in yourself. Your relationships with others are investments, your job is an investment, your environment is an investment, what you put in your mind and heart is an investment, your emotions are an investment—and the list goes on. When we make choices, there are outcomes, and those outcomes are the result of our investments.

Just as there are bad financial investments, there are bad investments we make with our health, our mind, our soul, and our emotions. You want to make choices that will yield high dividends. No matter what choice you make, even if it's a bad one with a really bad return, you can still get great benefits from it. Make sure you squeeze out of it all that you can.

Learn from your bad choices by learning why it was a bad choice to begin with. You will forever be a student in the school called life, where every experience, every person, and every situation is your teacher. If you pass the test, you won't have to repeat the same experience; if you don't pass, you will find yourself reliving the same situation over and over again, just with different people. Don't put yourself in a place where you are repeating the same course year after year. Learn from your bad choices and move on.

You must take responsibility for your life if you are to have the life you want and deserve. As an adult, this is something that you owe to yourself. Once you start taking ownership of your life and what happens to you, you start making better choices, you grow from every experience, and you start having the shifts you want and need in your life. No one can do this but you.

## Things to Think About

- Your life, your happiness, your health, and your mental, emotional, and spiritual state are all your responsibility.
- Stop blaming others for what you don't have. Start taking ownership for the things that go wrong.
- You need to do your part to have the life you want. No one else can do it for you.
- You make yourself responsible for your life by knowing and fully believing that no one can make you feel any way. You are in charge of your feelings.
- Master your mind by challenging your limiting beliefs.
- Take care of your body the way it was designed to be taken care of.
- Take responsibility for the choices and mistakes you make.
- Take responsibility for your emotional health by pursuing healthy, fulfilling relationships; seeing the positive side of things; establishing positive goals for yourself; and listening to your true self.
- Do your best to diminish the amount of stress in your life.
- Make good investments in your health.

# Choose Your Friends Right and Always Cultivate New Friendships

We all have a need to belong, to be appreciated, and to be loved. That's why friends are essential to our well-being. The people we choose as friends influence us in ways that we can't imagine. They can influence our self-concept, our self-esteem, the choices we make, and even our growth. So you can see that how you choose your friends is important.

There is a saying: "By your companions you shall be known." You are judged based on the people you surround yourself with. That's because we don't choose people who are very different from who we are. Even if there are noticeable differences between you and the other person, there is one or more commonalities between you two. Perhaps you've had similar experiences—you come from the same neighborhood and share the same values—or the other person represents someone you want to be.

The friends we choose are a direct reflection of how we see ourselves and who we are. If you have friends who are up to no good, who put you down, who don't have much to offer to you, seriously question the purpose of that friendship. What is it that you are getting from that friendship? How does that friendship make you feel? What does that friend represent? These are hard questions to ask, but they provide important insights that can help change your life.

Why is it important to choose the right friends for your well-being? Let me start by discussing what choosing the wrong friends does to you. We become that which we are surrounded by the most. If you surround yourself with people who have negative thinking, who don't have much going on in their life, and who put others down, you may condition yourself into thinking the way that they do. Your mind is like a sponge even as an adult, and it absorbs the messages that others transmit. You are not going to have great well-being when you surround yourself with people with limited thinking.

Those with limited thinking project onto others their thinking and feeling. How so? Well, they can only offer what they have, which is limited. They can only offer support based on what they believe, which is limited. Someone who doesn't know any better can't advise you any better. When you put a limit on well-being, you end up stuck—stuck in relationships that are not fulfilling, stuck doing a job you don't like, stuck with a life you're not happy with. Because you are surrounded by those with limited thinking, their beliefs become your beliefs, which further hinders you.

The people we surround ourselves with become our teachers. It is through others that we are exposed to different ways of being and living, and we form communities. The wrong friends expose you to things that can be harmful to you, like the wrong crowd and unhealthy habits. Anything that you are exposed to affects your well-being, so it's important to be aware of what is going on around you. On a daily basis, make it a goal to look for new and healthy ways of living. Try to be a little better than you were yesterday. Seek to grow in every way possible. You need friends who will help you in this endeavor.

What should you be looking for in a friendship? Most of us have similar needs when it comes to friendship; we want a friend who is honest and loyal, who loves and cares about us for who we are, and who has our best interest at heart. One thing I must add is that we need people who are positive in life and who are not constantly talking about problems.

A study published in 2008 in the journal *Hormones and Behavior* found that those who constantly talk about their problems with one another—the researchers called this "co-ruminating"— actually raised each other's level of stress. This is because it is indeed depressing to only talk about problems. There is so much beauty to life, and you want to surround yourself with people who, despite their problems, are still able to see that beauty.

Life presents each of us with many challenges; we don't need other people bringing us down with theirs. Now, when I write "positive people," I don't mean those who don't ever have problems and are not accepting of things that are not good in life. Not at all! Truly positive people take the good and the bad in life, accept the way they feel, accept the challenges, and try to make the best of it. It's not that you never talk together about your challenges or the sad things that are going on in your life, it's just that this is not the *only* thing you talk about together. What we talk and think about is what we magnetize and increase in our life, so pay attention to the conversations you have with your friends.

Because everyone is different, you may have different needs from a friend. It is normal not to mesh with everyone. There is nothing wrong with that. We are all different, so we're not going to have a strong friendship with everyone. Those who are ambitious in life, for example, need to surround themselves with people who are also ambitious. Just being a genuinely nice person doesn't suffice. This is because friends can fuel the person you are and who you are on your way to being. If you are trying to lose weight but your friends like to go out a lot and eat unhealthy foods, they will not be of any help to you in being the person you want to be. You need to find friends who are on the same journey or already like to eat healthy. Your personality and the journey you are on in life will determine the kind of friends you need.

It is my recommendation to strive to choose friends who want more out of life, who encourage you to be a better person, who are fully accepting of who you are, and who you know you can be 100 percent with. Have at least one person you can be your 100 percent with, anyway. You will notice as you meet people that you can't be 100 percent with everyone, and that's okay. It's important, though, for you to know what category to place that person in.

For example, there will be people you can only be 90 percent with, because they are not accepting of that other 10 percent of you. Some people will be good to hang out with, but you can't trust them with deepest secrets or everything going on in your life. That's okay too. There will be people you trust with certain things, but if you express an idea of yours they may ridicule you, so you can only be 80 percent with them. Not everyone is going to fit into the same category.

I'm not implying that you have to be different with different people. Not at all. You should always be yourself—but know that not everyone can handle all the things you are. We are all multifaceted; we have many different parts that make up who we are. You may be someone who loves to dance and social drink, but you also love to go to museums and read. Because there are so many different parts to who you are, it's a challenge to find someone who loves every single thing you love. Don't exclude someone just because you share only one thing in common. Don't expect one person to fulfill all those parts of you. Different people can fulfill different parts of you. There's nothing wrong with that. Open yourself up to having different friends. They can help you feel more fulfilled in the social aspect of your life.

Sometimes our disappointments with people stem from the fact that we didn't place them in the right category. We thought they were people we could be 100 percent with and then realized they are not. The disappointment comes from our own expectations. How do you know what category to place a new friend in? Only time will tell. Just take everything as bits of information that tell you who this person is. Please understand that the purpose of placing people in categories is not to judge them or anything of the sort. It is so you know how to be with your friends, because the truth is that not everyone will fulfill us in everything we may need as a friend.

Just as it is important to choose the right friends, it is equally important to cultivate new friendships all throughout your life. Whether you move to a new city or develop a physical condition that you didn't have before, always make it your goal to meet new people and make new friends. Sometimes when one develops a new condition, one isolates oneself, and this is not healthy for you. This is a situation where it becomes increasingly important to reach out to others who have the same condition as you do, because you can learn from one another and encourage each other.

Even if you're married or are a housewife or even a husband who stays home, maintain the friendships you currently have and cultivate new ones. We women, some of us at least, have a tendency to put aside our friends and tend to just the husband or kids. This is a big no-no. Different people and things play different roles. Your husband or wife plays one role, and your friends play another. This is where balance comes into play.

As we get older, our friends either get married; have kids so they don't have as much time as before to hang out with us; move (or maybe we move) so we can't see them as often; or pass on. For some, getting older is depressing; they see their lives change so much, and they lose friends because of life's normal process. One of the several reasons they feel this way is because they stopped cultivating new friendships and only kept the ones they had.

Although you must hang on to your old friends, keep creating new ones, too. This is part of your social health plan. This is where you are planning a lifetime of friendships, because that will add to your mental, emotional, and physical health. Having friends, especially as we get older, decreases our risk of mortality. Friends can even help alleviate stress, which contributes to heart disease. This is because having friends contributes to your sense of belonging.

Life is constantly changing, and having friends along the way is a must for your mental and emotional health. There have been studies that show a correlation between mortality and those with friends. According to a study published in the journal *Current Opinion in Psychology*, those who have a high quality and quantity of social relationships have a decreased risk of heart disease, high blood pressure, and mortality. So yes, it is very important to always keep cultivating new friendships.

How do you meet new friends? First, be yourself. There is no need to be anything other than yourself. You want to attract people who are like you and who resonate with you. Second, do things that you love. By you surrounding yourself with things that you love, you can know what kind of people you will meet and what kinds of activities or events they enjoy. Join a group or take on some volunteer work doing something that you will like. This will allow you to meet new people. You can't meet new people by staying home. Go out and, even if it's by yourself, do something you like. You will be surprised how many people you can meet just by going out doing the very things that you'd want to do even if you went by yourself. Don't wait for things to happen—make them happen.

Choose friends who are loving, caring, stimulating, and encouraging of your dreams and who you are. Choose friends who add to your life, not deplete it. Always make it a goal to cultivate new friendships. Taking meds isn't the only thing that should be part of your health plan. Part of it is taking action that contributes to your health. It is a must to always strive to build new friendships. You can meet friends everywhere and anywhere.

## Things to Think About

- Make sure to choose friends who are loving, caring, and supportive of who you are.
- Your friends play a big role in your overall well-being.
- Your friends can either add to your health or deplete it. Make sure you choose wisely.
- Different friends can fulfill different parts of who you are.
- Make it part of your health plan to cultivate new friendships.
- You can meet new people everywhere and anywhere.

# Choose Your Companion Right

One of the decisions we usually make very lightly is our choice of companionship. That's a huge mistake, because the wrong person can cause big, costly problems.

The person you choose is one you will spend most of your time with and trust with your secrets, your dreams, your money, your heart, and your well-being. Now, no one is perfect, and even your soul mate will have flaws. It's only normal that the person you love will get on your nerves at times, and you both will get mad at each other for silly things. Even the loveliest person can have a flaw. The question is whether it is a flaw you are willing to accept or not. If you can, meet each other halfway.

The person you choose will be the one person who is your best friend, your cheerleader, your helper, and your lover. This is the person you choose to form a home with, the person who will be the mother/father of your kids, the person you choose to respect and love. Because of all that this one decision implies, it is important that you choose wisely.

When you make this choice out of fear of being lonely or because you desperately want companionship or because you think that's all you can get—in others words, when you make this choice for all the wrong reasons—the result may be disastrous. You may end up feeling disappointed, in an abusive relationship, or having regrets with feelings of inadequacy. If you get married and stay together, you may make each other's lives miserable; if not, you may end up in a bad divorce. All of this could be avoided if you choose wisely.

For anybody reading this who is single and desperately wanting to meet The One, trust me when I say that I fully understand how you are feeling. The wait to meet the right person may seem so long. It's easy to fall into the trap of losing faith, losing patience, and losing hope of ever meeting the right person, but I now look at it this way: if my true desire is to get married and form a family, it is crucial that I make the right choice when it comes to companionship. It is much worse to get into a relationship with someone and end up with a very sour ending. Never lose sight of that bigger picture of what you truly want.

If you truly want to get married, have true companionship, and form a family, keep this want present in your mind. If you have to cut out photos of couples to remind yourself of what you want, then do it. Know that in order to get what you want, you must act and think on a different level. You have to be truly honest with yourself as to what your wants and needs are.

This will lead you to look at dating in a different way. Dating is a time for both of you to get to know each other on a deeper level and see whether you share the same values and goals and if you would be a good match. You don't have to agree on everything, but you must at least match on the things that matter most to both of you. It's important that you both can see each other together, can have projects together, and can see yourselves sharing each other's journey.

Dating is not a time to have sex when you're not in a relationship. Sex, although it is very pleasurable, was meant to "seal the deal" between two people, so to speak. The consequence of having sex before you are in a relationship is that you may end up becoming attached to someone who does not yet feel the same way you do. Your view of dating has to change if your goal is true companionship. What you do while you are dating has to be different.

When marriage is what you want, you have to look at things in the long term. You have to evaluate whether someone is trustworthy and really cares about you. Evaluate this person's relationship with his or her own parents and children (if any), and see if you share the same values and visions. You need to make sure this person can satisfy your needs and know if you will be a priority in this person's life.

There are many things to consider. Once you look at dating from this perspective, you will be able to make a better choice when it comes to a mate. Dating can provide you with a preview of what is to come if you enter into a relationship with this person. Choosing the wrong person for the wrong reasons is costly on so many levels, and so much hurt and disappointment can be avoided if only one enters the dating scene with the right perspective.

True companionship requires that you have a deep, true friendship where you both value each other's trust and secrets, and where you both encourage each other to be better human beings. As my soul mate friend so beautifully said, "Love allows for some wiggle room in that department" when it comes to some silly mistakes that we all make. When it comes to love, I can be quite impatient, but as my wonderful mentor said to me (I still call her my mentor since she was my mentor back in high school), "that love that you want takes time to develop."

It will take time for you to know and see if the person you are dating is your true companion. There will be tests that you both have to pass; life alone will provide these tests to both of you. Dating is a time for both of you to check if you are marriage material and if that's what you both want. You want to make sure the person you are seeing has the qualities you are looking for in a husband/wife and a father/mother for your children, and that you can see yourself growing together. There is a lot to consider while dating, so pay attention if your intention is something serious.

Choosing someone to start a family with is a serious matter that not only affects you and the person you choose but also affects your children, the children of your children, and your community. What forms a community are people and their families, and families are created at home. The way you raise your kids affects the way your kids see themselves in relation to others and their view of what a family is. For example, when a son grows up seeing his parents together in a healthy and loving relationship, that son grows up believing in the concept of family and the concept of marriage, and he will most likely have a healthy concept of the opposite sex. With this healthy concept, he will have a better chance of attracting the right person for him, because he didn't grow up with many issues that unfortunately we are starting to see in many homes.

One of the biggest mistakes women make when dating is to give the heart and body too soon. This is a big mistake, not so much because the guy may lose interest in you but because you are compromising your own well-being. It is too hurtful to go through that pain. We were not designed to go through that pain, but we do whenever we give our heart and body so quickly. The state of our heart influences our well-being in so many ways.

Your heart and body are two very precious things that you own. Treat them with care. Do not give them away too easily if your goal is to marry. The way dating works today is so wrong, and it only leads to unnecessary hurt. People are walking around confused about how to approach the dating scene. I am not trying to be a relationship expert, but as a wellness expert I do know that the state of the heart affects overall life and well-being. Your heart and body were meant to be given to that person who will cherish and love you, not to anyone who wants to just experiment with you. Listening to what today's world has to say about love and dating will only lead you to more hurt and will keep you from finding what you are looking for.

Men, when looking for a woman, make sure she will complement you, be your helper, and support you—and I'm not referring to the financial aspect, but to encouraging your dreams and walking alongside you. Two people who share the same values, dreams, and morals last long together.

If your goal is to find a wife, know ahead of time what it is you are looking for in a woman. Dating is not the time to be checking out how she is in bed. No, it is the time for you to know if she is the kind of woman you are looking for as a mate. It is time for you to check out her character and her values. Make sure you know what it is you are looking for, and make sure you do have the time to dedicate to a relationship. It is painful for both parties to get involved emotionally and then find that for whatever reason it won't work.

When you date people, pay close attention to what they are saying to you. Investigate what their visions are for life, where they see themselves in five years, and what their priorities are at this time. These are all things that indicate whether a relationship is even a priority for them, if they have the time to dedicate to a relationship, and if they see their future with you. Once again, this is not a time for you to be checking out each other's body or sexual prowess. Those are very superficial things and, in the end, they are not what sustain a relationship.

You want to make sure the person you choose is someone who can be your best friend, because as you both get older, sex will not be a high priority. If you don't have a strong friendship as a foundation, your relationship will crumble, because you won't have anything to talk about. It is important that you both can grow together; this is why you need to know what that other person's visions are for their life. It's sad when a couple divorces because they grew apart. This is why communicating while you're dating is a must. Make sure this is someone you know you can communicate with about everything and anything.

View dating as a job interview, because in essence it is. You are trying to figure out if you are a good match. When dating, one of the most important elements that you need to have is discernment. What does this mean? You have a sense of clarity of who you are and what you want and need from a companion. You don't have anything blocking the goals you have in regard to what you are looking for in a relationship. You don't have anything keeping you from seeing what is in front of you. You don't have anything clouding your emotions.

The person you choose as your companion plays a critical role in your overall well-being, because this is the person you are choosing to form a home with. This is the person you are choosing to be the mother/father of your children. You are trusting this person with your heart, your body, your secrets—with everything for that matter. This person has the capacity to elevate you or destroy you.

As I discussed earlier, your home needs to be an oasis. This is the person you are creating a home with, so you both need to create an oasis. If this person brings chaos into your home, guess what, it is going to spill all over your life. The people you choose to be around the most have the greatest effect on your mental, emotional, spiritual, and physical health.

It's so sad how the divorce rate keeps going up each year. There are many factors to this, but one of them is that I don't think both people took enough time to get to know each other very well before marriage. Such lack of discernment can happen to anyone. I know it has happened to me. If the person you are seeing is only interested in finding out whether you are sexually compatible, this is not the right person for you. I want to clarify that I'm not suggesting that a sexual connection is not important, just that it should not be the basis.

I compare the body and the heart to the legs of the table; these are some of the things that help you keep standing. When one of the legs of the table breaks, the table can't stand. Same thing with the heart and the body. When the heart is compromised, other areas of your well-being get compromised as well. When you give your heart away and that person doesn't have the capacity to take care of your heart the way he or she should, your whole well-being will be affected. When your heart doesn't feel good, you don't feel like eating right, and you don't feel like taking good care of yourself. You may not even want to do the things that you once enjoyed doing. This is so unnecessary. You had no business giving your heart away if the other person didn't make a commitment to you to begin with and show you that he or she had the capacity to take care of your heart.

Men, if what you are looking for is a wife, make sure that the woman you are seeing is wife material and looking to form a family. You want to know that your well-being is a priority for her. She should be willing to support you in your journey and goals, to walk alongside you. You are looking for someone who cares that you are taken care of, cares how you present yourself to the outside world, and cares to make your home an oasis.

I'm not saying that it's women's role to take care of men. All this the woman will do because she cares and she wants to do this. When you love someone, taking care of that person and being there for him or her is something you do out of love, not out of obligation. How you feel is going to matter to that person.

I cannot forget to add that both women and men need to make sure that the person they are dating is willing to do the work it takes to maintain the relationship. Relationships take work. They are not meant to be easy breezy. You're both going to be challenged from time to time. You both are going to get on each other's nerves. This is because, and you need to remember this, you are two different individuals no matter how much you love each other. Embrace those differences, because it is your differences that can help balance out the relationship.

Women, you want to make sure that the man you are seeing will be a provider, will protect you, will make your well-being a priority, and will make you feel safe and loved. Be sure this is a man who has a good head on his shoulders, has his finances together, has his life together, and is looking for an equal. You need a man who shares your same values and visions—someone who complements you and adds to your life.

Make sure this is a man who is responsible and has a job that he loves—someone who has his life put together. There is a reason for this. Men who don't have a job they really enjoy or feel their life is not put together will not even think of a serious commitment. If what you are looking for is a committed relationship, don't waste your time with a man who does not have this as his intention. Listen very carefully to the things he says; one way or another, he will reveal his true intentions to you.

Also, beware of a man who has been recently divorced, since you don't want to be a rebound. He may not be ready for what you are looking for. Pay attention especially if he is still hurt by a divorce. I don't care how nice he may be or how much he is marriage material, it won't work because he is not ready for a committed relationship. Just because he says he wants a committed relationship doesn't mean that he's ready for one. You really want to have your eyes and ears open.

You need to know who your potential mate is mentally, emotionally, and spiritually. Both of you want to find out each other's goals, aspirations, and if he or she would be willing to move wherever you move. You do not want to find out after making a commitment that you want to move but the other person is unwilling. This will create a conflict.

Ask questions. Ask many questions. Ask as many questions as you can. Whenever the other person says something that raises a question in your mind, then certainly ask it. Remember, you want to learn as much as you can about this person, and you can only do this by listening and asking questions. Dating is like a job interview. You are trying to figure out if this person is fit for the position of being your companion.

## Things to Think About

- The person you choose as a mate can either be an asset or a liability.
- Make sure that you are not choosing someone for all the wrong reasons—because you just don't want to be alone or just want companionship.
- This one decision not only affects your life but the life of your children (should you have kids with this person), the children of your children, and your community.
- Choosing the wrong person is so costly on so many levels, most of all to your well-being.
- Dating is like a job interview. Ask as many questions as you can.

# Communicate More and Choose Your Words Wisely

**M**any people don't communicate the way they should. Lack of communication leads to misunderstandings, misinterpretations, unnecessary hurt, and broken homes and relationships. For this very reason, it is crucial for you to communicate more with others and to choose your words wisely.

When relationships and homes are broken because of lack of communication, the well-being of everyone in the household is compromised. That's because peaceful, harmonious homes and relationships are key to being able to feel in balance, recharge your own batteries, and face the jungle, which is what I call the outside world. As I discussed earlier, when your home is chaotic, you will carry that chaos everywhere you go. It's sad to see how many relationships and homes are broken because of a lack of communication—and sometimes where there is communication, words are not chosen correctly. The wrong words and lack of communication create a territory of misunderstandings, misinterpretations, and unnecessary hurt. We were all provided with the ability to communicate, so let's utilize that ability wisely.

There are many consequences to poor communication. Not communicating with someone can lead to that person thinking things that perhaps are not the case, but they can't seem to avoid thinking those things because what is really going on is not being communicated. This is especially true in romantic relationships. Lack of communication leads to needs not being met. If you don't communicate what you need, what you want, and how you are feeling, how can the other person know how to help you and be there for you? Nobody can be a mind reader, and so it is important to express your needs, wants, and feelings clearly.

Lack of communication breeds mistrust, because when we don't communicate with our loved ones, it is as if we start to no longer know them. Lack of communication creates division and distance. What unites people is time spent together. When time is spent together, there is a certain level of communication that goes beyond just words. Time spent together communicates presence, caring, importance, meaning, and love. When this is what you communicate to people, you start building bridges—strong bridges that no amount of wind or storm can break apart. That's how powerful communication is.

Communication goes beyond words. There is also the nonverbal aspect that you have to look into as well. When you speak, you have to pay attention to your tone of voice. Your body language matters. Even when you're sending a text, it's much more than a text. An email is much more than an email. A phone call is much more than a phone call. I think if people paid more attention to this, there would be stronger bonds and, at the end of the day, happier people. This is because part of well-being and optimum health is the relationships that we have with others.

When you create strong, genuine bonds with others, there is a sense of comfort, a sense of belonging, and a sense of meaning. We all need to feel that we are meaningful to someone. That's a basic, healthy, normal need. We are emotional and social beings, and because having strong, genuine bonds is so necessary for our mental, emotional, and physical well-being, it is a must to remember that you are one of the parties responsible for making that happen. You do that through communication.

When communicating, be present. There are households where it seems like everyone is in his or her own bubble. No one asks others how their day went. They don't even bother to engage in the other person's world, and this creates division. This makes you distant, and where there is distance, there will be miscommunication. Miscommunication leads to lack of love, ill feelings, feelings of emptiness, and alienation.

If you live with your family, make sure that you are involved in the daily life of your loved ones. Ask them how their day went when they arrive home. Be interested in what they do, what they are thinking, and their goals in life. The interest that you show creates a bridge. It lays the foundation for a strong relationship. What forms a relationship is the bond you both have, the memories you all form together, and the feeling of connection and presence. It creates an attachment between you two that will be hard to break. You want to form these bonds with your family, and it is best to form them early on. Having this kind of communication creates a sense of attachment.

This kind of communication creates healthy relationships. Healthy relationships are needed for a healthy life. I feel that nowadays we live in a world where we are so hungry spiritually, and I think this hunger stems from a lack of meaningful relationships. One of the things that hinders meaningful relationships is ineffective communication. Communicating effectively leaves a legacy of love, connection, and health. Make sure to leave this legacy with others.

Another aspect of communication that many overlook is the listening part. I think many of us do more hearing than listening, and there is a difference between the two. Hearing is more about the physical, mechanical aspect of what the ears do—the picking up of sounds. Listening is more of a process. You hear what the person is saying, and you mentally process what it is that you heard so that you can get to a point of understanding that person's point of view. When you are listening, you are doing your best to get to a point of empathy, meaning that you feel and understand where the other person is coming from.

When you reach this level of understanding, miracles happen in relationships, and the way you respond to that person changes. You no longer come from a place of hurt or anger. When you communicate, you are able to let the person know where you are coming from without brushing off how he or she feels, and you are able to effectively express your feelings as well.

This is how powerful effective communication can be. It can revive relationships that seemed to be doomed. It unites people, and it creates a stronger love. If you think about it, what makes someone want to be close to you is the connection he or she has with you, and that connection comes from communication. There is no way around it.

Something I would like to add when it comes to communication is how important it is that you choose your words wisely. The wrong words can hurt, leave scars, and kill or severely damage emotions and relationships. When hurtful words are said, they are out in the open. There is no way for you to take back what you said. When you say something really hurtful to someone you care about, those words can actually kill any feelings the person may have had for you.

I know that for those who are passionate like me, it can be a challenge to hold back when feeling hurt, since we want to just get off our chest what we feel, but the best thing to do when feeling overwhelmed with emotions is to just step back. Wait until you no longer feel as emotional as you do, and think about what you're going to say. Think about the motive behind what you want to say, and ask yourself if what you are about to say will get you the result you want.

What happens when you speak in the heat of the moment is that you may say what you feel right then, but it may have effects that you did not intend. In the end, a feeling of regret weighs more than not expressing all the anger and hurt you feel. A lot of those negative emotions can be diminished through effective communication. There is no need to express so much hurt and anger all at once.

How can you start communicating more effectively right now? Start by listening instead of hearing and talking. Give the gift of your time and attention to those you love. Through this gift, you communicate presence. You communicate that these people matter to you, that you think of them, that you love them, and that they are meaningful to you. You expressing this will mean the world to those you love and will only strengthen the bond you have. Showing that they are meaningful to you is the greatest gift you can give. It is the gift of love and health. If you ever question what you have to offer to others, remember this.

Make sure you use loving words with others and think before you speak when feeling angry or hurt. Make an effort to keep the connection with those you love. It's not how long you converse with someone, it's that you want to let them know you thought of them. Send a text letting them know that you miss them. You will be surprised how this one text speaks volumes. Now, if every time you communicate with them is through texting, something is seriously wrong. Reserve texts as a way to let others know that they are still on your mind and that you miss them. Texts were meant as a way to keep a connection, not as a primary mode of communication.

Nowadays, there are so many ways to communicate, there is basically no excuse for not maintaining a connection. Start now to communicate more effectively with those you love. Listen more.

Choose your words wisely. You never know whose day you might brighten with your presence.

These are the ways you build up communication, however, there are several things that break communication down. One of the biggest is *not* listening. When you hear but do not listen, you'll never understand where the other person is coming from. Listening is a process; it requires you to pay attention to what is being said to you. When others don't feel understood by you, they feel disconnected. Disconnection kills love and severs bonds.

Listening requires you to put aside for a moment your own thoughts and feelings. I'm not implying you should ignore your feelings—just put them aside so you can fully listen to what the other person has to say. When you are busy paying attention to your thoughts and feelings, you are engrossed in your inner self. There is no way you can listen to someone else when you are doing this. You need to be available to tune in to what the other person is saying and where he or she is coming from.

Another communication-breaker is being uninviting in your way of being. This means there is something about your energy, your way of behaving, the way you express yourself, your body language, or your facial expression that keeps others from approaching you and starting a discussion. If you've noticed that your communication with someone has broken down, pay attention to your role in this. Often in a marriage, one spouse doesn't feel able to approach the other to discuss thoughts and feelings. That perspective colors the way you view that person.

Body language, gestures, and the energy you put out are so important when it comes to communication. They all play a role in the way others view you, and their view of you determines how they relate to you. It's true that you can't always control the way others react to you—because at the end of the day no one has control over another person—but you can control the way you behave and what you put out there. Do your best to be inviting so that others feel they can approach you.

How can you start being more inviting in your communication? Pay attention to the feedback you are giving with your facial gestures and body language. You may not realize how these reactions give away your thoughts and feelings about what the other person is saying. Even if your gestures and body language mean nothing to you, they are still being received as feedback. Paying attention to all of this is going to seem like a lot of work at first, but over time it will get easier.

Another way to be more inviting in your way of communicating is by listening to other people's feedback and ask why they feel that way. If they are telling you that they don't feel understood, their explanation as to why can help you learn what you can do differently. There is a Spanish saying, *hablando se entiende*, that means it's by speaking that one can be understood, so allow others to express why they feel the way they do. Do your best not to judge those feelings and perspectives. Judging breaks down communication, and you want to build it up. Remember that what creates a bridge for communication is openness and understanding. When others feel understood, they will be more willing to open up to you, creating trust and closeness.

Confront the person you're conversing with if something is said or done that doesn't sit well with you. That sounds negative, but believe it or not, confrontation can foster understanding and closeness. The book *Confronting Without Offending* by Deborah Smith Pegues truly changed the way I view this issue. Pegues explains that confrontation is only negative if you approach the other person in a negative way. Don't be afraid to confront someone when there is a problem. Confrontations are a necessary component to healthy relationships. If you never express how you are feeling and thinking, how are others supposed to know how their actions make you feel?

As human beings, we will always do things we don't mean to do that are hurtful or bothersome to others. As Pegues states in her book, confrontation is merely two or more people coming together face to face to discuss something. If you care about your relationships, be open with the other person and get things off your chest so the other person has a chance to explain. If you care about the relationship, keep two-way communication open.

Be supportive of the people you're communicating with. There is something about providing support that creates closeness and trust. Support also glues the other person to you. You can be more supportive by, once again, doing your best to not be judgmental and making sure the person feels understood. Being supportive is not joining others in their sadness or misery if they feel that way. It is encouraging them to be their best, believing in them, and cheering them up when they need it.

The intimacy a lot of us look for comes from effective communication. Effective communication is healing. It restores marriages and friendships; it restores order; it encourages love; it even helps you to do your work better. It builds a strong foundation that no amount of wind, turbulence, or storm can break down. Effective communication is so much more than just speaking—it is choosing your words carefully, listening so that you can understand where the other person is coming from, being aware of what you are communicating with your body language, making an effort to know how the other person feels, and being inviting in your way of being. I guarantee you that if you communicate more, and more effectively, your relationships will blossom and so will your overall well-being.

## Things to Think About

- If you are the type of person who keeps to yourself, why do you think this is? Can you find a way to communicate more with those you love?
- Have you shown your family and loved one that you love them in a way that makes them feel loved? If not, how can you start doing so?
- When you get angry or frustrated, take a step back and wait until you cool off. Think about what you want to say and your reasons for wanting to say it. Will what you are about to say bring you what you want? If the answer is no, then don't say it.
- Once words are said, you can never take them back. The way you communicate can unite or divide.
- Communication goes beyond words. It includes body language, actions, listening, and trying to understand where the other person is coming from.
- Strive to always communicate love to others, no matter who that person is.

# Embrace and Adapt to the Changes in Life

Depending on where you are in life, accepting and adapting to change can be difficult. However, it is a must if you are to maintain well-being. The reality is that life is about constant change. Life is not stagnant. It comes in different stages; there is a course life takes whether we like it or not. We grow; we get older. Those around us get older and have lives they must cultivate. Their lives change and we must accept that as well. Don't base your happiness on outside things, but on yourself. It must lie within you, not on whether this happens or that happens.

Refusing to accept or adapt to change can be very damaging. When you resist, you can't mold yourself into the circumstance you are currently living in. One example that hits home for me is the story of a wonderful friend who used to live in the same building as me. She was always a very happy, joyful person with a passion for life. She was aging, but I sensed that she didn't accept that fact. At the time of her death, I was surprised to learn that she was in her eighties. Even though her body showed her age, her spirit didn't. Her feet would hurt, but she refused to give up her high-heel boots and high-heel shoes. She felt dizzy often and should no longer have been alone at home, yet she was a strong woman with a youthful spirit.

Her downfall—which I know led to her death—was that she didn't want to accept the changes in her life and the fact that she was aging.

Had my friend accepted the fact that she was aging, she would have changed her shoes to flats or sneakers. She would have looked for help and gotten someone to live with her so she was not alone at home. She would have accepted that she gets dizzy, and in order to avoid a deadly fall, she would have bought a chair to the shower in order to avoid slipping. This is what accepting and adapting to the changes in life allows you to do. You think of alternatives so you can enjoy the stage you're in.

When you don't accept and adapt to change, you become rebellious to the point of going against the current. As a result, you are unhappy, clouded mentally and emotionally, and unable to see the options available to mold to your current situation. Your well-being is compromised.

How do you accept the changes you're going through when you don't like those changes? I believe the first step is just to be aware of the changes, from the changes your body is going through to changes in relationships as people move away or move on. Be observant so that you will always know what the situation is. I know this doesn't sound hopeful, but resisting doesn't help.

The second step is to remember that it is *you* who makes you happy—not a circumstance, not a person, not an event. Outside things can certainly add to your happiness, but ultimately happiness is a choice. Waiting for a circumstance or event to change or waiting for someone to arrive or do something is very dangerous to your well-being. You are postponing your happiness. What if nothing happens or changes? Are you going to continue feeling miserable because of that?

You can't afford to do this to yourself. By focusing on what might happen, you are missing out on all the greatness that is right in front of you. You may be overlooking wonderful opportunities that are just waiting to be noticed. There is no benefit to postponing your happiness. This is why your happiness needs to rely on you and nobody or nothing else.

How can you start relying on yourself for your own happiness? Think about the things that make you happy. Look within yourself for the answers you need. Think about the person you want to become. Visualize the life you want. You can't imagine how many times from my parent's home I would visualize myself drinking coffee on my balcony—a balcony I still didn't have, but that the universe surely had in store for me, because I've visualized it. There is something about visualizing that soothes the soul.

Believe and know that you have everything it takes to make yourself happy. Think about those things you want to achieve and what you can start doing now that will get you closer to those goals. You'll notice that you feel good after completing tasks that contribute to your goals.

Do something every single day that makes you happy. Discipline yourself to think happy thoughts. When you notice your mind wandering around, and you notice that you are starting to feel sad or negative, stop yourself and start again to think happy thoughts. Your thoughts are something that only you can control. Your feelings are something that only you can control. Others may be able to influence the way you feel and think, but only if you allow it.

Another way to start relying on yourself for your own happiness is to see how valuable you are. There is a big correlation between your own happiness and the way you view yourself—your self-concept. If you can't seem to get a good perspective on yourself, take a moment and mentally step aside. View that person you stepped away from— meaning your own self—and ask yourself what you think of that person. What are some of the things you see in that person that are great? What makes that person you are seeing attractive? What are some traits you find amazing about that person? What potential do you see in that person?

If this mental exercise is not working for you, get a photo of yourself in which you look absolutely amazing. Imagine this person is not you. The point of doing this is to get you to see that individual's potential and then to recognize that this amazing being is you after all. This exercise can be powerful because it is easy to see the potential and greatness in someone else and challenging to see it in our own selves. In this exercise, you see yourself from a third-person perspective. Finally seeing how amazing you are will increase your self-esteem and help you trust yourself and believe you have what it takes to be happy.

I do recognize that in order to know that you can rely on your own self for your happiness, you must first trust yourself. Trust is something you must work on every day. Self-concept and trust go hand in hand, so a healthy self-concept is another must for well-being.

Another way to accept the changes in your life is by considering what you may want to tweak in your life to make change easier. Is there something in your life you must accept that you've had a hard time accepting? As time passes by, it's important to recognize that there are adjustments that can make the changes you are going through a bit easier. We humans tend to be a bit resistant to change, so you're not the only one who finds this not so easy.

Remember that nothing lasts forever in life. Everything is borrowed. To put it bluntly, you have an expiration date. That being the case, there's no point in becoming attached to things. Appreciate every moment you have been given. Every one of those moments is precious. Learn to live in the present moment. The past is a beautiful memory, the present is full of happiness, and the future will be blissful. This should help you keep things in perspective.

Do your best to enjoy every stage of your life. It is a privilege to move from one stage to another—one that not everybody gets. Think about how you went from kindergarten to elementary school to junior high school to high school. You couldn't stay in high school forever, otherwise how would you grow and enjoy all the other things that life had for you?

View every stage of life as an opportunity to grow and become a better version of you. With every stage in life comes growth and the opportunity to see another side of yourself that you probably didn't think was within you. Remember that your perspective on everything is what makes up your reality in life and determines your course of action. Make sure you have the right perspective.

The moment you start embracing the changes around you and adapting accordingly, you will feel differently about your life. You will see that regardless of the changes that are occurring in your life, you can find something to be happy about. You can recognize the beauty in things even when they are not the same. The moment you embrace and adapt to change, you will start another chapter in your life in the right way. Just as it would be boring to remain in the same chapter of a book, after a while it is boring to remain in the same "chapter" of your life. I encourage you to start viewing your life stages as chapters to look forward to and embrace as new learning experiences.

## Things to Think About

- It is crucial to your overall well-being to embrace and adapt to the changes in your life.

- Our life goes through many stages. Nothing ever stays the same.
- Rely on yourself for your own happiness.
- Learn to be happy no matter what the circumstances may be.
- What is your self-concept? Is it healthy? If not, what can you do to change it into a healthy one?
- Try to see yourself from a third-person perspective so that you can see how amazing you are.
- Every stage in life is an opportunity for growth and to see another side of you that perhaps you didn't know was there.

# Get a Mental and Emotional Detox

A detox is so good for you, especially when your body has accumulated so much junk. Many people know about a physical detox, but have you ever considered trying a mental and emotional detox? Just as your physical body accumulates junk, so can you accumulate mental and emotional junk.

A mental and emotional detox is about eliminating thoughts, beliefs, and emotions that do not serve you but hinder you, slow you down, and take away from your health. To me, there is no exhaustion worse than mental and emotional exhaustion. These can make you more tired than physical exhaustion. When your exhaustion comes from your mental and emotional state, it starts eating your body up slowly. That is a fast track to depression and anxiety, and I'm not saying this lightly. This is why a mental and emotional detox is a must.

I recommend doing a mental and emotional detox one or two times a month, depending on how much mental and emotional junk you've accumulated. In this way, you can keep your emotional and mental state in check by assessing your thoughts and beliefs as well as how you are feeling about yourself and your life. When assessing, try to identify the thoughts, feelings, and beliefs that no longer serve you.

When having negative thoughts, feelings, and beliefs, it is

important to learn where they're coming from. The reason you want to understand and know this is because when you can get to the root of something, you can find a permanent solution to the problem. It is equivalent to dealing with an illness by treating the root problem rather than the symptoms. During the detox, I encourage you to understand where all these are coming from.

Don't just brush disturbing feelings, beliefs, and thoughts under the rug; they will all come back sooner or later. If you deal with an illness by only treating the symptoms, the illness itself may remain dormant. While the symptoms appear to be under control for a time, they come back and perhaps they are worse.

Detox may be an uncomfortable process. Digging within yourself to figure out how things feel is not a lot of fun. You will have withdrawal symptoms, just as you would with a physical detox. There will be moments when it feels like too much work to look within you and figure out where your thoughts, emotions, and beliefs come from. There will be times when you will want to go back to your old ways because they are familiar to you.

This detox will require your constant effort. Well-being takes work, but without it, you cannot have the life you want. Making the mental and emotional shift you need will not be easy, but I can guarantee you that those who are mentally and emotionally fit, as I like to say, are constantly working with their mental and emotional self. They are monitoring their mental and emotional state, they are aware of their thoughts and feelings, they challenge their way of thinking, they always do their best to better this aspect of their life, and they are constantly feeding their mental and emotional self with positive food. They guard their mind and heart from being contaminated with negativity.

It is easy nowadays to be contaminated, mentally and emotionally. If you are not careful, you will be bombarded by things that bring you down and make you look at the world in a negative way. This contamination can come from the media, from your own environment, from people who drain you, and from beliefs that you have adopted but in reality belong to other people. It is very important for your well-being not to allow your precious self to be contaminated.

Guard your heart and mind, and only fill up with beautiful and positive thoughts, and loving and encouraging words. If you are used to listening to negative things, filling up your mind and heart with positive and loving words may be a challenge at first. It will take some time, but you're worth it. I suggest that during this detox, you surround yourself with those who truly love and support you. Let them know that you are doing a mental and emotional detox so they can support you on your journey.

During this detox I also suggest that you do things that bring you peace and joy, whatever that may be. This will help with the withdrawal symptoms. I also encourage you to have a journal. There is something so helpful about writing things down on paper, so that thoughts and feelings become more real for you.

If your negative thoughts, beliefs, and emotions are so incredibly strong that you cannot do this detox on your own, I suggest you see a therapist or psychologist. This is not a sign of weakness; on the contrary, it is a sign of strength, because you can admit that you need help sorting things out. When you need help, it is important to get help. You will not regret it. Sometimes life throws situations at us that can be overwhelming, and there is nothing wrong with getting a little assistance.

Babies need to learn to crawl before they walk, and during this process they fall. You will do the same when challenging negative thoughts, feelings, and beliefs and replacing them with positive ones. You will fall at times when trying to be a better person. You still have to push yourself through, despite your failures. Falling and failing doesn't mean you can't do what it is that you are attempting, just that you have some more learning to do.

Be particularly aware of your emotions during this time. We are emotional beings, and most of our decisions are based on emotions. We are wired to either seek pleasure or avoid pain. Sometimes we make the mistake of seeking pain subconsciously and not even being aware of it. We seek pain when we get ourselves in situations that we know are not healthy for us—including bad relationships, questionable decisions, and foods we know our body cannot handle. Detox is a time for understanding these actions and why you do them. Revelation leads to great changes. Harmful actions come from somewhere within us that is hindering our greatness. It is important to challenge this and understand the purpose behind your actions. Your emotions are an asset, but they can also be a liability.

Positive emotions lead you to make decisions that are conducive to good health. Negative emotions lead you to make decisions that take away from your health. This is why you want to keep your emotions in check. Your emotions can be a source of inner guidance if you allow them to be. No emotion, not even a negative one, has to be a bad thing. This is why I write that during the detox, although you are eliminating negative emotions that don't serve you, before you eliminate them, you want to understand them so that you can make a positive use of them.

You are going to treat your emotions like you would with a child, with tenderness and care, because in essence you are caring for your true self, which is your soul. You are going to ask it questions to figure out where these emotions are coming from and why. You are going to ask yourself what it's going to take for you to feel differently. Have this chat with yourself.

I know this may sound crazy—and I am not saying you will have a talk with yourself out loud in public. You are going to take

116

some quiet time for yourself with no interruptions and nothing else to do but sit down and spend time with your thoughts and emotions. This is another form of self-care. When you tend to your emotions, you are taking care of your soul. You are going to do for yourself what you would do for your friends, supporting and encouraging them. Anything less than this is not conducive to getting the results that you need from this detox.

Thoughts can have a life of their own that we are not aware of. The mind can run away and do its own thing. We need to keep our thoughts on a leash just like our dogs so they don't run away and hurt others. Our thoughts can actually do harm if they are negative.

During this detox, be aware of what your thoughts are doing during the day. If you need to write in a journal what your thoughts are, then do so. Understand where your thoughts are coming from. If they are negative thoughts, ask yourself why you are having these thoughts. What is their purpose? The brain is one fabulous, powerful organ, and it is the one organ we do have the capacity to manipulate. Your thoughts affect your emotions, and because of this you must understand why you think the way you do. Power comes not just from education but also from understanding. The more you understand yourself, the greater the changes will be.

Many of the great things we want to achieve in life must first be achieved in the mind. Our mental and emotional self must be right before we can achieve anything—and this "anything" includes relationships, good eating habits, and a prosperous business. Everything starts within you. When you are not right mentally and emotionally, when your mind and emotions are full of junk, everything around you will reflect that. Stay fit in these areas with mental and emotional detox.

## Things to Think About

- Have a mental and emotional detox one or two times per month.
- The purpose of this detox is to keep your emotional and mental state in check by assessing what your thoughts and beliefs are as well as how you are feeling about yourself and your life.
- Detox may be an uncomfortable process, because you will be digging within yourself to figure things out, but in the long run it will benefit you.
- If the process is difficult and you seem to fail, no worries— just keep at it.
- Be aware of your emotions, since emotions are feedback from your soul, which is your true essence.

# Get Yourself Financially Fit

I am not a financial expert, nor do I want to be one. Still, none of us can ignore how important our finances are to our well-being. It can be very stressful to know that you are running out of money. It can be very stressful to know that you don't have much saved up. It can be very stressful not to make much money. It can be very stressful to not have enough to feed yourself or your family, or to barely be able to pay the bills or the rent, or for both you and your partner to have to work in order to make ends meet and as a result, you can't be there with your kids as you would like to be.

When it comes to our finances, it is important to be financially responsible, to be financially literate, and to learn the value of money. Financial responsibility implies that you are aware of how much you make. You are aware of your expenses and keep track of them. You spend your money wisely on things that actually matter, and you understand why you are spending the way you are.

One thing to avoid is something that I think is more common for women than men—emotional shopping. I did this for several years because I was trying to fill a void I felt, but in the end I had the same void and more debt. Recognizing and avoiding emotional shopping can keep you from getting yourself into unnecessary trouble, such as accumulating things you don't need and getting yourself into debt. This kind of spending is very irresponsible; I know this was very irresponsible on my part. This is why I say that in order to be financially healthy, you need to be financially responsible.

I personally believe that working for an hourly wage eventually leads to poverty, because unless you are working—meaning you are physically on the job—you are not making any money. Although it can be nice to work for someone else, there is nothing like working for yourself and doing something you truly enjoy. Working for yourself has its challenges—everything has its challenges—but making money doing the things that you truly love is unbelievably fulfilling. If you have a job you love, even if you are working for someone else, the mere fact that you love your work is great. You will not feel like you are working and this is healthy. It is important to choose a job that you love and enjoy.

In order to increase financial health, you must be financially educated. Learn about the different ways you can invest your money. Start contributing to a 401K the moment you start working. Don't wait until you are in your thirties to do this. Start as soon as you can, because every little bit does add up. It may not seem this way in your early twenties, but time does fly, and you don't want to feel like you have to catch up and make up for what you didn't contribute. That can be quite stressful. If you didn't contribute to your 401K and you are in your thirties or forties, it's not too late to contribute.

Also put some money aside in your savings. Create an emergency fund with at least six months' worth of expenses, or half of what you make in a year. This is the least that you should have in your emergency fund. There is something comforting about having an emergency fund; should anything go wrong, you have at least a six-month cushion. If you can put more into your emergency fund, by all means do so. The more you put into that fund, the better. Create another account you can access anytime you want for things you may need. This way, you're not tempted to use your emergency fund.

When you start educating yourself about finances, make sure you consider the different ways you can make money. Chances are you are not taking advantage of all the opportunities that are actually out there. You might be surprised to learn that starting your own business doesn't have to be that expensive. There are several ways you can have your own business—like, for example, direct selling, so you are sharing with others products you love and that others will love and will buy. A franchise is another possibility. Educate yourself in this area, because nowadays it is necessary to have other sources of income. You don't want to rely on just your job.

Investment is another way to be financially wealthy. I suggest you invest wisely, not just on businesses or property. Don't forget that even you are an investment, so make sure you eat right. You may be asking yourself, "What does that have to do with my finances?" Here's the answer: when you are sick and physically compromised, you don't have the energy to work the way you are supposed to. You become a liability to yourself and to others. Be an asset instead. Your body is an asset, and you protect that asset by eating right.

Make sure that every day, you are fueling yourself efficiently. No junk food, no overly processed food, no frozen meals on a daily basis. Give your body what it needs so that it can give you what you need: energy, strength, and endurance. Your body is perfectly designed, so try hard to keep it that way. Feed it all the nutrients and vitamins it needs. When you are physically healthy and fit, you are going to be fit to work, especially if you have a job that is very physical. If you don't want to be jobless, you sure better take care of yourself to be healthy.

Spending a little extra on healthy food is not a waste of money; it is an investment you are making on your own behalf. The better you feel, the better you can do your job, the more you can give of yourself, and the more hours you can work. Look at the way you are taking care of yourself as an investment in your financial health and future. Even if what you are buying may be a little costly, it is so cheap in comparison to how expensive it is when you are sick.

Another good investment you can make is in your education. I know education can be quite expensive, but look at it this way: the more you know and the more skills you have, the more valuable you are as an asset. You can start opening doors for yourself and creating other opportunities that can lead to a better paying job and greater financial health. Don't view education as a waste of money; look at it as an investment you are making in yourself. The more skills you have, the more value you will have for the market, and the more doors can open up for you.

Always try to open more doors for yourself. You never want to be stuck or stagnant. Times change; make sure you keep up with the technological changes that occur. Depending on the kind of job you have—and even if you have a job that doesn't require you to learn certain things—still learn them. You never know when what you learned may serve you. Nothing has to go to waste. Your education doesn't have to go to waste. It never does. Education is never a waste of time or money. Even when two subjects may seem unrelated, everything is somehow connected. What you learned can serve you for either the job you currently have or a future one.

One of the ways to apply things you learned in school—and a great way to increase in value for the market, increase your skills, and become more of an asset—is volunteering your time in something that is meaningful to you and allows you to learn and grow as a person. You grow as a person by doing this since this allows you to learn so much about yourself, and you are also networking. It's through networking that you learn about other opportunities that are out there and get recommended for them. You can never go too far by yourself; you always need other people. Volunteer work is also something you can add to your résumé. How cool is that?

Don't forget to read books on finances. There are plenty of books out there to read. When it comes to your finances, what you do on a daily basis adds up to success for your future self.

## Things to Think About

- Finances greatly affect your well-being.
- Strive to be financially fit by educating yourself as to the different ways to make an income.
- Start contributing to your 401K if you haven't already.
- Create an emergency fund and have a savings account where you can touch that money should you need it while leaving your emergency fund alone.
- Invest in yourself in every way possible, especially when it comes to your health.
- Consider volunteer work in something that interests you so you can use the skills you have as well as learn new ones.

# Know Your Value and Role as a Person No Matter What You Do

Some may mistakenly think that they don't have much value because perhaps they didn't go to college, may not have many skills, don't make much money—whatever the reason may be. Please know that this is not true. You have so much worth, and your value comes from something so much deeper. Why do I mention this in this book, and what does it have to do with your well-being? Once you recognize the value you have and the role you play—not just in your life but in other people's lives—your actions will be different, your words will be different, the choices you make will be different, and the way you care for yourself will be different. There is something so powerful about knowing your value that transcends and creates a ripple effect even on those around you.

I would like to present some examples to you of what I mean with all that I am writing. When you understand the value you have as a mother, you know that everything that you do and say is setting an example for your child. You fully understand that you are one of the pillars of your home. As a wife, you understand the role you play in your husband's life as the support system for him, in helping him be the man he was meant to be.

For those who are fathers, when you fully understand the value you have as a father, you understand that everything you do and say is setting an example for your child. You are teaching your son how to be a man and a father. You are teaching him what a home is supposed to be like. You are teaching your daughter what she should expect from a man who is courting her. In essence, you are impacting the relationships your children will choose in their life for the future.

Many do not realize that the responsibility of living life fully is a big one, and one to take seriously. It affects generations to come, and it affects the way people feel. You do not need to be famous or have money to be important. You already are important because of the impact your life has at this moment.

As a friend, your friendship is impacting someone right now because of your presence, your words, your encouragement, and your existence. I think back then, the reason why there wasn't that much need for a therapist is because the friendships people had were so therapeutic. There is something so healing about genuine bonds; there is nothing like it. So do you realize how important your friendship is to others? Start noticing the impact you have.

For this very reason, it's important to do your job at work right. Someone else is impacted by what you do, no matter what the job is. A job wrongly done can cost others their smile, their money, their safety, their vacation, their dreams—so never think that what you do doesn't matter. It may not matter to you because you are not doing what is in alignment with what your soul wants, but don't underestimate the importance of the job you do.

For those who are single, who haven't started a family yet, you still have so much value to others. If you aspire to have your own family, everything you are doing while you are single will impact that future family. When you start working on yourself, doing things that fulfill you, and going for your goals, you will have so much more to give to your future family. You will learn things you can share with your future kids. Because you are filling your life with so many positive things, you will be a better role model for your future family.

Now is your chance, as a single person, to make sure you are fit in every way. You do this by pursuing things that make you happy and fulfill your soul. Start seeing your value now, and know that if you aspire to have a family, who you are now will impact them greatly.

Know that your value comes from who you are on the inside. It comes from your true essence, which is your soul. It comes from all that you have to offer from your heart and mind. Your time is valuable, your words are valuable, your thoughts are valuable, your work is valuable, your experiences are valuable, and what you have to offer as a person is valuable. You have more than enough qualities that make you valuable to the world, but in order for the world to see that value, you first have to be able to see that value yourself. Once you are able to value yourself, you will know your worth, and you will not waste your time with anything or anyone who cannot see that worth.

When you understand where your value comes from, you will appreciate your well-being more, and you won't allow any circumstances or people to compromise that. Your well-being is fundamental to being your most valuable self. Place yourself in situations that add more value to you as a person so that you can serve others in a greater way. Only allow people and situations that add more happiness to your life, make you smile, make you laugh, make you feel loved, and make you feel great because of who you are.

I encourage you to start seeing your value no matter who you are, what job you do, or how much money you make. Remember that your value doesn't come from external things; your value comes from within you. You have to see your value first. You are worth your weight in gold, and your worth is shared through your work, your friendships, and your family. We all have something of value to share with others; it's just a matter of taking notice and appreciating it. I encourage you to take the responsibility of living your life fully.

## Things to Think About

- It is important to know your value.
- You are worth so much more than your skills, than your job, than the money that you make. Your value comes from something so much higher than anything material you may own, and more than anything that you feel you may lack.
- The responsibility for living your life fully is a big one, and it must be taken seriously.
- Someone is impacted by the things you do every day.
- It is your responsibility to make sure that you are fit, so that you can have more to offer to others.
- Knowing your worth is central to your well-being in every way.

# My Final Tips

There are many other "little things" that are not so little when you think about them, because they all add up to creating a lifetime of wellness. One of the things I would suggest you keep in mind is that well-being is something you are always striving for. It has no end. It is not something you work on for now and then stop once you get it. Well-being and wellness is a journey; everything you do, eat, think, say, and give matters. You are the sum of what you do on a daily basis.

In this chapter, I'll share some of the things I recommend that I didn't mention in other chapters. One is to have a home library of books you can read that either make you feel good or teach you something. This home library will reflect who you are and who you want to be. A book can be a good companion if you let it. It's like having that author as a friend speaking to you and advising you. Books stimulate your brain and keep you entertained.

I also recommend that you always strive to learn new things. Fall in love with learning. I believe that education should not end the moment you graduate. The world itself is a school where everyone you meet and every experience you have is a teacher. By allowing yourself to be a lifetime student, you grow in every way. This growth allows you to become a better and happier person. At the end of the day, I'm pretty sure you want to become that kind of person. Learning is a way to nurture both your mind and soul.

Make it your goal to be a giver from the heart. I write "from the heart" because one should not give with the intention of receiving right back. That kind of giving is not sincere. When you give from the heart, you do not expect anything in return. Rather, you give because you have in abundance. Being a giver from the heart will also help attract to you more positive people, but beware of those who just want you to give to them without receiving anything in return. Giving to the wrong people can actually suck your energy dry, and you do not want that.

Although you should try to be a giver from the heart and not expect anything in return, be careful who you give the most precious gifts of your time and your heart to. There are those who love to receive these gifts but don't offer themselves in return, and this can feel like a blow to you. Be careful to protect these major assets of yours. It hurts to give them to those who can't see the value.

Have healthy boundaries for yourself. When you do, you won't allow others to step all over you. You won't allow others to disrespect you. You won't allow others to take privileges that don't belong to them. Having healthy boundaries is like having a fence—not a wall, but a fence—where you draw the line of what is acceptable and what isn't, what you're going to allow in your life and what you're not. It's about protecting your property, and that property is you and your well-being.

There are times when the unhealthy relationship is with yourself. This is one of the most destructive and hurtful relationship you can have, because it will reflect on everything you do and have in life. It's important to have healthy boundaries with yourself so that you do not say or do anything harmful to your overall well-being. There are times when we get in our own way and hurt our own life. Sometimes we are the ones polluting our mind and emotions, and this is why it is important to establish healthy boundaries for ourselves in order to keep this from happening.

Learn more about who you are and how you function. When you understand yourself, you can do things that work for you because of this level of understanding. For instance, if you function better with a routine, you know you are a structured person, and so you do things accordingly. The more you learn about who you are, the more understanding you will be toward yourself. When you understand who you are, you know where you are coming from and why you feel the emotions you feel, and you can modify and act accordingly. There is power in getting to know and understand yourself.

Live with courage. Life is to be lived fully, and in order to do this, you must be willing to stretch yourself—meaning that you are willing to grow. You will have to go through changes, and changes are not always easy. There is a lot to get used to and a lot of resistance you must overcome. Have the courage to go after the things that perhaps others aren't brave enough to go after. Have the courage to be your real self, to go by what you feel, to go after what matters most to you, and to go by what you believe in. Go boldly against the current rather trying to fit in. Have the courage to be everything you can be and the courage to look within yourself and see who you really are.

Life is about courage, because the lack of courage can make you live a life full of fear. A lack of courage can leave you mentally paralyzed and even physically paralyzed, unable to see all that is in store for you and everything you are capable of doing. Courage is required in order to live life to the fullest and to be the best you. The only way to get that courage is by doing. Part of living a great life full of well-being is exercising the courage muscle.

If you are intrigued and want to try something, why not go for it? I think it is more scary to go on with life not doing what you want to do. It feels lousy to get older and live with regrets because of the things you didn't do. Without courage, we would live a meaningless life; we would live according to what felt comfortable and what we were used to doing, but not everything that feels comfortable is right for us or up to par with what we truly deserve and are capable of. You only have one life to live, so make sure you live it fully. Dare to do the things you desire to do. Dare to learn that skill you think is impossible. Dare to chase that dream of yours.

Whether you are chasing a dream or looking for true love or trying to lose weight, whatever it is, exercise patience. This is one area in which I must admit I struggle. I'm very impatient when it comes to love, but it takes time for true love to develop. I know what you're probably thinking: you wish it was different, but this is the way it is. What happens when you lack patience for whatever it is that you want is that you rob yourself of the chance to see its fruit. Time is the only thing that can tell you how fruitful something will be. So let time take its course and tell you what is what.

Practice having compassion toward others. Each and every one of us has a story, and we all have our baggage. Some people's baggage is heavier than others. You never know where other people are coming from when they behave the way they do. Instead of judging, try to be understanding.

I think if we were to practice more compassion, there would be more tolerance and harmony. By practicing compassion, I'm not saying that you're going to excuse bad behavior from others should others behave in a way that is unacceptable, but at least you can look at that behavior from a different perspective than anger or resentment. Although the person's behavior doesn't change, the way you feel about what happened will change with this change of perspective. Practicing compassion keeps you from taking what others do personally.

For true healing medicine, go to nature. Nature has provided so many ways for us to add well-being to our life, and the best part is that it's free. Laughter is free and so healing. Hugging is free, and there is something so soothing to the soul when we hug someone. Love is the most powerful and necessary of all the emotions. It is essential to survival, so love more.

Enjoy the outdoors. Being close to nature keeps you grounded. I can go on and on, but the point is to go to the things that truly give you ultimate well-being. We all want well-being, we all need it, but you have to go to the right sources to get it. Looking in all the wrong places just makes you feel empty and lost.

Remind yourself every single day of your passions. In this hectic world we live in today, it is so easy to get lost in everyday things that don't matter that we forget what our true passions are. Remind yourself of your passions in a way that works for you. Either have pictures that remind you of where you want to go in life or use words—whatever works for you. Without passion, if you're not careful, a part of you can feel dead. In essence, it *is* dead, since there is a part of you that is not being nurtured. When you don't nurture your soul, there is no way to be happy, and happiness is part of well-being.

Practice the art of letting go. There are times when we hold on to things that no longer serve us, relationships that are no longer healthy, and a past that no longer is the present, just because of the memory that we hold of it. Holding on to these kinds of things is not healthy for you. They make you stuck and keep you from looking forward to all the goodness that is yet to come. You are a prisoner in your own jail that you are creating for yourself. When you hold on to things that are not serving you, this holding on magnifies negative feelings or thoughts you may have. It makes you blind to all the goodness you currently have, and it makes you miss out on what life has for you right at this moment.

Holding on to things that are not good for you in the end makes you a loser. You lose your happiness, you lose your peace, you lose your faith, and you lose your well-being. Being at such a loss doesn't help you move forward. It doesn't help you feel better about life or yourself. I think letting go is an art, and for many, including myself, not an easy one. When you learn to master this art, you will feel free. You will feel light. You will open yourself to new possibilities and better things yet to come.

What is the best way to let go of things? Start with the small stuff. If you don't know how to let go of the small stuff, it will be even harder to let go of bigger stuff that has meaning to you. When something small like not being able to find what you really wanted at the store bothers you, start by thinking that perhaps it wasn't meant for you. Practicing this mentality will help you build the trust and faith muscle that is so crucial in mastering the art of letting go.

One of the many reasons it's hard to let go is a lack of faith that something better can come along. I do think letting go takes a high level of trust and faith. It is important to trust that things happen for the best and have faith that something better will come along. It's important to trust that the universe is conspiring for your best. This is the kind of thought that will help you release anything that isn't working in your favor, whether that be in regards to love or a job that you wanted to anything in between. Without this trust, the fear that this is the best you can get will haunt you and make you hold on to things that don't even come close to what you deserve. This ends up hurting your overall well-being, which I'm sure you do not want.

Anything that makes you feel bad and anyone who makes you feel less than happy is not worth holding on to. Nothing is worth holding on to if it robs you of your peace. For this reason, I encourage you to start working on those trust, faith, and letting-go muscles in order to get yourself mentally, emotionally, and spiritually fit.

Start seeing the value within you. I know I wrote a chapter on this, but it's worth repeating. You are a valuable being, no matter what anybody says. The faster you realize this, the faster your life will change in the way you deserve and want it to.

When you do not see your value, you settle for situations and relationships that are less than what you deserve. You act in ways that only feed this false idea of yourself as not worthy, when indeed you are. When you don't see your own value, everything in your life reflects this feeling. You not only see this in your relationships with others and in the situations you are in, you see it with finances and your relationship with food. It's as if when you can't see your value, you don't appreciate your body the way you should, and you don't feel you deserve financial abundance. Not seeing the value within you is too costly to your overall well-being.

You start to see your value when you realize all the valuable things you have to offer. I am not referring to material stuff, I'm referring to what you have to offer about yourself. Your value goes beyond your physical attributes. It is more about who you are as a person.

Think about some of the gifts you have to share with others. What are some things you have to add to other people's lives? What is the state of your heart and mind? Nurture yourself, nurture your body, nurture your soul, and don't ever compromise your peace. Do things that make you happy. Surround yourself with people who see your value. This also helps you see your own value, because there are times when we do feel sad and fail to see our value.

Know where your focus is, and focus on what truly matters. This helps you stay grounded, centered, and in balance. When you are centered, you can react more effectively to circumstances. You don't come from a negative place but from a calm and peaceful place. When you focus on things that really matter, you focus on the things that provide greater fulfillment. You don't feel a void in your life. You don't feel the need to look outside of yourself, and so you don't fall into temptation as easily. You start being in control of your life.

One of the many reasons people lose control in life is that they don't have a real sense of what they want. They don't use their time and energy on what really matters, because they are not aligned with what matters most to them. They don't take the time to be centered and have stillness. Moments of stillness are so important. These are moments where you can gain valuable information from your soul that can lead you to the life you want.

Stillness is where you gain insight into what you must do in life. It is where you are able to listen to your inner wisdom. There are different ways you can learn to be in stillness, and one of those ways is through meditation. You can even try yoga. The point is to have moments of stillness where you are quiet and listening to your inner guide. This is what provides you with all the answers to your questions.

Give yourself breaks when needed. We are human beings, not machines. We live in a world where so many of us numb our feelings and thoughts and just keep going and going as if nothing else matters. When we numb our feelings and thoughts, it is only a matter of time before we explode. As a human being, you are a social and emotional being with needs. When feeling hurt, give yourself a break to feel the hurt and grieve if you have to do any grieving. Just don't remain in that hurt for too long. You don't want to wallow and spiral down until you hit rock bottom—that is not healthy.

If you are working too much, make sure you take time to stop and smell the roses. Often we work so much that we forget and neglect the things and people that matter most. When we don't take breaks, we get all caught up in the little things and live in our own little bubble, neglecting the big things that are most important in the long run.

Appreciate and love those who truly love you. It's amazing how much we tend to take for granted those who truly love us and accept us just the way we are. Take time to cultivate those relationships. Let those who you love know that you think about them and love them. Life is too short to focus your attention on those who don't see your value and don't give you the time or day. You just never know when it may be your last time to tell that person how much you love him or her.

Healthy relationships are truly a good investment. Think about it: right before you leave this earth, you will not be thinking about your job, how much money you made, or the material stuff you own. When times are bad, it is those who truly love you—those people you have invested time and energy in—who will be there for you. A job will not be there for you, nor will that beautiful car you bought.

It is important to put into perspective what really matters in life. In the long run, putting value on things that don't really matter hurts your well-being, because it leads to mental and emotional poverty. There are many ways to be rich in life, and one of them is by cultivating healthy relationships and leaving a legacy of love.

Set goals for yourself. Goals give you a sense of purpose and keep your mind occupied. Going after goals makes you stronger and gives you a sense of accomplishment, which raises your self-esteem. What gives life meaning is living with purpose and having a purpose. Goals help you do this.

It's sad that many people live day-to-day, letting their lives pass them by. They don't feel that sense of accomplishment. Only you can give it to yourself. Start thinking about the things you would like to accomplish now, and start setting goals for yourself.

Remember that you are not meant to be living day-to-day—just getting up, going to work, going back home, and going to sleep. This is not the life you're meant to live. This is probably the way society is telling you to live your life, but it is not how you are supposed to live. You are meant to be happy; you are meant to have goals; and you are meant to be living a meaningful life. You should be striving for that every day.

Why is this important to your well-being? Feeling like you don't have many choices in life is very depressing. To be conditioned into thinking that there is nothing to life other than getting up, working, going back home, and going to sleep puts you in a state of helplessness. This is a negative state to be in, and it leads to a mentality of poverty in every sense of the word. You don't want that for yourself! Part of well-being is happiness. You are meant to be happy. It is your birthright.

Guard your heart and spiritual self. Many times it's because we don't guard these parts of ourselves that we get into so much trouble. When your heart and spiritual self isn't right, your whole life suffers. I believe that a heart and spirit in pain slowly kill you. The hurt is like a cancer that spreads to all parts of you. It invades your thoughts, and your thoughts affect your actions. Your actions, when they are not the right ones, only feed negative emotions. You don't feel the kind of love that you are supposed to feel when you are in a negative state, and this lack of love leads you to not take care of your body the way you are supposed to. Lack of love leads to you not being loving toward yourself, which only hurts your well-being.

Many things can compromise your heart and spiritual being. One of them is disappointment. Maybe you're disappointed with yourself or because of a situation or person. Disappointment is a part of life, so it is important to learn how to deal with it. The best strategy is to change your perspective of the hurt you feel by drawing upon the lessons learned and becoming a better person.

When you have been disappointed when it comes to love, for example, look at it as the universe conspiring in your favor. Your best revenge is becoming a better version of yourself than when you were with that person. From every disappointment, learn to be better. Let every day that passes make you into a more attractive, mature human being. That is what you were meant to be.

Be aware of your needs. Many of us don't realize how strong our needs are, to the point that they blind us into making bad choices. There is nothing wrong with needs; they are part of life, and they are to be respected and acknowledged. However, if your needs are not in check, they can rule over your thinking and feeling, and they may prompt you to do things you wouldn't otherwise do. Needs can actually turn you into a person that you are not.

Balance in everything is important. One of the best ways to balance out your needs is by making your sense of peace and well-being a priority. No matter how much you may want something, judge whether it is worth having what you need based on how it makes you feel and whether or not it adds to your life.

A perfect example is the need to be in a romantic relationship. That is a normal need, but when you make your sense of peace and well-being a priority, you are a better judge of whether a potential partner is worth having in your life. You are not so hungry for romance that you put it before everything else. The problem with needs is not the need itself, but the intensity of that need. Feeling hungry is normal, but when you are starving, even a salty meal tastes yummy. When peace and well-being are your priority, you'll never settle for something that is bad for you.

Like your needs, your fears are something you have to learn

how to manage. Don't let them stop you from doing what you want. Facing your fears is something you build little by little, like muscles, and every step you take counts. That's how you gain strength and self-esteem. The best way to manage fear is to remember that everything at first feels scary because it is unknown. Do your best to view fear as excitement. The greater the goal, the more you may feel it, but it can motivate instead of block you.

Whatever you want to do, know that it is important to take action. Otherwise, you are only dreaming, and you will remain in misery. Nothing can be achieved without taking action. If I had never taken the action of setting time aside to write, make corrections, and follow through on my publishing company's suggestions, this book would never have come into existence. It's the same with that weight you want to lose—unless you take the time to cook your meals, make better food choices, and work out, you will not get the results you want.

If you never write that résumé, look for opportunities, and send your résumé to different places, you will not get the job you want. If you never decide what you are looking for, and put yourself in alignment to meet the right person, you will never have the relationship you want. Everything requires action. The moment you accept this, you will start moving toward that well-being you are striving for.

A lifetime of wellness is possible, but it requires effort. It is my sincere desire that this book will lead you to think about your life and how to make it better; that is my intention with my coaching, my blog, my writing, and my online radio show. Each and every one of us is meant to live a great life. Start living the way you were destined to live. It is up to you to make this happen.

## Things to Think About

- Assemble a home library of books that either make you feel good or teach you something.
- Strive to be a giver from the heart.
- Have healthy boundaries for yourself.
- Learn more about who you are and how you function. There is power in getting to know and understand yourself.
- Exercise patience. Waiting is the only way to know how fruitful something will be.
- Practice compassion toward others.
- For true healing medicine, go to nature.
- Remind yourself every single day of your passions.
- Practice the art of letting go.
- Start seeing the value within you.
- Know where your focus is, and focus on what truly matters.
- Take time to remain in stillness.
- Give yourself breaks when needed.
- Appreciate and love those who truly love you.
- Set goals for yourself.
- Remember that you are meant to be happy, to have goals, to live a meaningful life, and to do your best to live this life.
- Guard your heart and spiritual self.
- Learn from every disappointment.
- Face your fears.
- Be aware of your needs.
- Remember that no matter what it is that you want, you must take action.

# References

The Better Sleep Council, http://bettersleep.org.

Byrd-Craven, J., D. Geary, A. Rose, and D. Ponzi. "Co-ruminating Increases Stress Hormone Levels in Women." *Hormones and Behavior* 53 (2008): 489–492.

Dement, William C. *The Promise of Sleep: A Pioneer in Sleep Medicine Explores the Vital Connection Between Health, Happiness and a Good Night's Sleep.* New York, NY: Dell Trade Paperback, 1999.

Maas, James B. *Power Sleep: The Revolutionary Program That Prepares Your Mind for Peak Performance.* New York, NY: Harper Collins Publishers, 1998.

Pegues, Deborah Smith. *Confronting Without Offending: Positive and Practical Steps to Resolving Conflict.* Eugene, OR: Harvest House Publishers, 2009.

Reblin, M. and Uchino, B. "Social and Emotional Support and Its Implication for Health." *Current Opinion in Psychology*, vol. 21, no. 2 (2008): 201–5.

Waller, Pip. *Holistic Anatomy: An Integrative Guide to the Human Body.* Berkeley, CA: North Atlantic Books, 2010.

Made in the USA
Lexington, KY
03 July 2017